A Incomplete Family History

From Picardy to Bethnal Green and beyond

A.R.Polain

Copyright © 2022 by A.R.Polain

All rights reserved. This book or any portion thereof may not be reproduced or used in any manner whatsoever without the express written permission of the author except for the use of brief quotations in a book review.

Edition 1, 20th November 2022

Contents

PART ONE – THE FAMILY

1 CLAUDE POLAIN – (1701-1756)

1.1 Historical Context 3
A move away from the established Church 3
The Consequences in France 3
The Consequences in England 4
Timeline 5
Famous People 5

1.2 Claude's Family 6
Claude's parents 6
Claude and Barbe 7
Claude's children 11

1.3 Bits of the Jigsaw 13
Puzzles and explanations 13
Claude's Will 13
Spellings 14
Claude's birthplace today 14
18th century London 15

2 ROBERT POLAIN (1744-????)

2.1 Historical Context 19
Life in the 18th Century 19
Timelines 20
Famous People 21

2.2 Robert's Family 22
Robert and Ester 22
Robert's Children 23

2.3 Bits of the Jigsaw 24
Robert, the son of Claude? 24
Church Records 24
Church Attendance 24
Addresses and Trades 25

3 PETER POLAIN (1774-????)

3.1 Historical Context 27
A Changing World 27
Timelines 28
Famous People 29

3.2 Peter's Family 30
Peter and Mary 30
Peter's Children 30

3.3 Bits of the Jigsaw 34
Food for the masses 34

4 GEORGE POLAIN (1809-1849)

4.1 Historical Context 35
A window on the past 35
Timelines 36
Famous People 37

4.2 George's Family 37
George and Elizabeth 37
George's Children 39

4.3 Bits of the Jigsaw 41
Education 41
Slumming 42
Campaigning 43
Slum Clearance 44

5 JOSEPH POLAIN (1849-1893)

5.1 Historical Context 47
A Growing City 47
Timelines 50
Famous People 51

5.2 Joseph's Family 51
Joseph and Maria 51
Joseph's Children 51

5.3 Bits of the Jigsaw 52
Puzzles and explanations 52

6 *GRANDPARENTS*

6.1 Historical Context 55
End of an Era 55
Timelines 57
Famous People 58

6.2 The POLAIN family 59
John Albert Polain (1876-1958) 59
Jane Holloway (1878-1939) 59
John & Jane's Children 61

6.3 The STEVENSON family 63
William Henry Stevenson (1876-1940) 63
Florence Stevenson (1880 - 1962) 70
William & Florence's children 73

7 *PARENTS*

William Alfred Polain (1912 - 1991) 74
Violet Ivy Stevenson (1915-2016) 78
Vi and Bill's children 80

PART TWO – LOOSE ENDS

Crime & Punishment 83
Samuel Polain 83
Eliza Polain 87

Missing in Action 88
Albert Edward Polain 88
Victor George Polain 89

"Polains" in the Middle Ages? 92
Introduction 92
The storm clouds gather 93
The War starts 95
Present Day 97

PART THREE – REFERENCE

APPENDIX A

The 'Old Nichol' 101
- Life in the 'Nichol' 102
- Half Nichol Street 103
- Life and Death in the Nichol 106
- "Sanitary Ramblings" 107
- "Ragged London" 109
- Faces from the 'Old Nichol' 116

APPENDIX B

Photographs: A technical note 119

APPENDIX C

Weaving: Linen, Silk and Cotton 121
- Types of fabric 121
- What is Cambric? 122
- Why it matters to us 123

APPENDIX D

The French Hospital 125
- The Pest House 125
- The French Hospital 125
- Present day 126

APPENDIX E

What was (is) a Calvanist? 127
- Who was Calvin? 127
- What does a Calvinist believe? 127
- Who are Calvanists? 128

APPENDIX F

East London Churches 129
- A Tale of Three Churches 129
- French Churches 130

 Spitalfields Churches 132
 Stepney Churches 133
 Bethnal Green Churches 135
 Shoreditch Churches 138

APPENDIX G

Unidentified Persons... 141
 Births 141
 Marriages 142
 Deaths 142

APPENDIX H

Maps & Diagrams... 145
 Polain Family Homes and their Surroundings 147
 Edinburgh, Scotland 148
 Bethnal Green, London 148
 Threadneedle Street (Bank), London 148
 Sample Census Forms 148
 Simplified Descendents Chart (inside cover) ....

A Brief & Incomplete Family History

Preface

Why ?

I have no intention of dropping off the perch anytime soon, but recent events have demonstrated that the unexpected can happen anytime. Even when events are expected, there is a natural tendency to put things off until the last possible moment.

I am therefore conscious that if I was to disappear without warning, all the work I have done on the POLAIN family history would be lost. Not that this would be any great loss to mankind, but future generations of the POLAIN family may find this little potted history of interest. By common consent, it appears that an interest in your family background gets more relevant the closer you get to meeting your maker. So whilst the following pages will have little to interest the younger family members now, there may well be those of a certain age that could be interested.

How?

Most of the information in this document that is specific to the POLAIN family is managed on a PC. However, like many similar programmes they can be difficult to navigate and interpret. This family history has therefore been structured to show a clear ancestral line between Claude POLAIN in 17th century France, to Violet and Bill POLAIN in London in the 21st century. I have also attempted to include general information about the periods so the reader can see the family within its historical and social context.

I know my limitations

In some aspects I cannot hope to do the subject matter justice. In particular the life of the inhabitants of 'The Nichol', whilst well documented in easily accessible sources, is probably outside the comprehension of someone used to regular meals, double glazing and central heating. If you find what I have written to be even modestly interesting, I suggest that you look at the original news reports or read the book *'Child of the Jago'*. I found the contemporary records to be fascinating and horrific and far better written than I could hope to achieve.

Caveats and Explanations

This is a work in progress. I have had photocopies, notes, maps and other documents laying around for a long time but have only recently started collating them into a form suitable for others to see. This document cannot be viewed as an accurate historical record as I haven't used sufficient academic rigueur in its preparation and have frequently omitted to record the sources of some of the information.

Confusion can easily happen. Frequently the eldest children have the same first names as their parents. Some siblings will have the same first names, but switched around (James William and William James). Sometimes John will be known as Jack, sometimes people use their second name instead of their first. The same person can have two different names - Absalom appears at some stage to have been known as Abraham. He can only be positively identified by the name of his wife.

Sometimes, complete families disappear. We have records of Absalom's children's birth, but no records at all after that time. Maybe they moved to an area where church records no longer exist, maybe they moved back to France or maybe they all died. On the other hand, family records may reappear after a generation or two, but by that stage it is next to impossible to link the individuals into the family tree with any confidence (such as Samuel POLAIN who was sent to prison for theft).

In putting the tree together, I have concentrated on the male line. This has been for practical purposes as the POLAIN females would change their surname on marriage and without access to the marriage certificate it isn't possible to continue tracing their family. In the same way, it is not easy to identify the maiden name of girls that marry into the POLAIN family. In some cases this also causes problems, such as the Workhouse records, where widows would frequently revert to their maiden name.

Certainly, some of our ancestors were illiterate and dates of birth are frequently approximate. Marriages are sometimes recorded but less than might have been expected by the number of births. Records of deaths are of limited value as these records don't contain any family data that would be useful. Over the last few hundred years, the POLAIN family have typically had large families, but with such a high infant mortality rate, it is unclear how many of the children would have lived until adulthood and had their own family. It is probable that a lot of the child deaths would not have been recorded before the start of formal registration in 1837. Death records are also prone to the problem of 'familiar' first names being used, rather than formal first names (I can't imaging many of our ancestors knowing what was on the record of their birth).

Until the start of formal registration of births, marriages and deaths, we have to rely on parish records. These seldom survive although in our case the POLAIN family history seems to have been well documented by three main churches; The **French Protestant Church** in Threadneedle Street, **St. Matthew's** in Bethnal Green and **St. Leonard's** in Shoreditch. Records from these churches have survived from the 18th Century and indexes, digitised copies and translations are available on line.

See **Appendix F** for details of these churches.

The quality of contemporary documents improved over time, together with the quantity of information contained in the records. The earliest census records, in 1841, contained only limited information but by 1911 the census included useful information such as address, family relationships, numbers of children not surviving etc.

On the other hand, there are many records that survived that have limited value in preparing a family history, except for the most ardent researcher. Included amongst these are the early Land Tax records (which are in effect just lists of names but with no information that can be used to tie the individual into the family) and workhouse records (which are poignant but of limited use). It contributes little if we know that a Liz POLAIN was senile when she entered the workhouse if we can't determine if she was connected to our family. It also appears that reliance on the Work House was a transitory situation for many people, who we presume were suffering short term financial difficulties. Frequently people would enter the work house and discharge themselves after a few weeks or months at their own request as their situations improved.

The use of the phrase *'born' (or married or died)* ***about*** *1900'* may cause confusion at first sight. This is a consequence of the way that the registration index works. Births, death and marriages are collected and published four times a year in an index. From the Index, it isn't possible to know the actual date of the event more accurately than within the preceding 3 month period. The actual date can only be found by applying for a duplicate birth, marriage or death certificate. For individual cases, this approach is justified, but with a large number of records such an approach is impractical and costly. In the case of death certificates, little information is shown on the certificate for the family genealogist.

For anyone living in modern London, it seems strange to be looking for events that happened in Bethnal Green in the *'**Middlesex**'* records. Historically, the southern boundary of Middlesex was the north bank of the Thames, so many Victorian or earlier records refer to events in the East End of London as being in Middlesex.

Until 1889 and the establishment of the London County Council (LCC), local administration had been carried out by the local parishes and counties. When the LCC was set up, they also formed 28 metropolitan boroughs.

Street Names

I cannot begin to count the wasted hours I have spent trying to track down streets using the name given in the contemporary records. I had hoped that by visiting a specific location, known to our relatives in the past, that I would feel some connection with them. But it isn't to be-certainly not in London.

Since the Saxons started developing London on the ruins of the Romans, the city has been in a constant process of rebuilding, redevelopment and reuse. First the canals cut huge swathes through the city, followed a hundred years later by the railways. Now, car use has increased and the roads need widening to cope with the traffic. Inner city industrial areas have all but disappeared, with buildings either demolished or replaced by housing or the buildings retained and the area "Yupified".

Street names change with the fashions and are soon replaced. After the Battle of Trafalgar, London was awash with streets named after Nelson, Collinwood and their fellow commanders. After Waterloo there was a similar effect. But these names too fell out of favour and a redeveloped street was always a prime target for a new name. In the same way, New

Castle Street (or was that Newcastle Street?) may, or may not, be anywhere near Old Castle Street, but it really doesn't matter too much as all will have had their names changed within 50 years, and the streets demolished anyway. Present day streets don't always follow the same line and route as their predecessors, even if the name is the same.

If there was a public house in the street called 'The Cock' (or one of a thousand names) the street became known as 'Cock Lane'. Presumably when the pub closed or changed name, the street name, over time, would follow suit.

Then there are the red herrings. I found a photograph of Trafalgar Street on the internet. It was described as being about 1870 and in 'The Nichol'. I found an old fire insurance survey map of the Nichol about 1890 which identified where Trafalgar Street was (at the east end of Half Nichol Street). I was convinced I had a photograph of the street where George and Elizabeth POLAIN lived in 1849. But on further inspection, the photo and the map didn't match up. The pub had the right name (The 'Lord Nelson', obviously) but was in the wrong place-and the houses didn't match the description and height given in the insurance survey. After days of fretting and trying to get to the bottom of the puzzle, I just had to give up and accept defeat. I had been guilty of trying to force a square peg into a round hole-clearly the photo had been mislabeled at some point, or maybe it was a different 'Trafalgar Street'.

Many streets in different areas of the city originally had similar or identical names. As the city grew and travel became easier, it became necessary to rationalise the street names. For instance there were over 60 streets called 'Cross Street' spread across the city. Probably more called 'Church Street'. The rationalisation was carried out between 1857 and 1929. In addition, many street names were lost during the blitz of London's East End, never to be re-used.

There are indexes for street name changes available on line and I can guarantee many wasted hours trying to track down nonexistent streets if you try this line of investigation.

Looking for the 'old' Bethnal Green

You will hunt in vain for the 'old' Bethnal Green our ancestors lived in.

Poor quality housing tends to have a short life, so the houses, generally whole streets, tend to get rebuilt frequently. Demand for housing grew as rural workers migrated to the urban areas seeking work. 2 storey houses get rebuilt into 3 storey houses as they hold more people. Then 4 and 5 storey houses become more common as land prices increase.

As the Industrial Revolution changed our rural landscapes, it also changed our urban landscape. Staple products were mass produced in the city. Without constraints on pollution, it made sense for the centres of production to be close to the major markets. Housing for the factory workers grew up around the factories. Factories grew up, expanded then disappeared as market demand ebbed and flowed. Workshops were replaced by factories. Factories were replaced by housing and housing was replaced by factories. So a never ending circle of development, reinvention and redevelopment continued in the East End of London.

New industries were created. The gas works needed fuel, so canals were cut through the towns and open countryside. The Regents Canal was built so that coal could be delivered to the gas works to the north of the city. The Hertford Union canal linked it to the Lea navigation. Industry grew up along the sides of the canals, then housing for the factory workers.

As the city grew and expanded into the suburbs, the volume of traffic through inner London increased. Road widths increased, routes changed, junctions took up more space. This accelerated as people moved from horse drawn transport to motor transport. Train lines into Liverpool Street and Broad Street from the east of England cut through whole swaths of housing in the East End.

And then came the Germans. The damage they did in the First World War was minimal (there were Zeppelin and Bertha raids over London in 1916 and 1917) but the real damage was done in the Second World War.

Kids these days have grown up in an age of precision strikes, laser guided bombs and limited collateral damage. In 1940, things were a lot different. Bombing was inaccurate and the East End housed the London docks and the industries that supported them. In short, Bethnal Green became a legitimate target, with whole areas obliterated overnight.

And after the German's had gone away, the Town Planners took over and destroyed what remained.

Don't get me wrong-the living conditions for people in Bethnal Green in the 1920s and 1930 were probably not much better than during Victorian times i.e. terrible. No doubt a lot of Bethnal Green was dramatically improved during and immediately after the war. Temporary housing (the prefabs built on bombsites all over London) was a huge improvement in living conditions for many in the East End.

It is almost impossible to find anything of the old Bethnal Green. Occasionally you may find a building that our ancestors may have recognised, but these are few and far between (the most obvious being the churches). Occasionally, walking round the East End you will see a building with a date, or a label giving the buildings original function, which will give you a clue of what the past looked like.

To give an example to how the area has changed, the map below shows Warner Place where our family lived in the late 1800s and early 1900s. The road is still there in the recent aerial photograph, but all the houses have gone. Where once there was high density housing, now there are parks and open land. And as it is within walking distance to the City, the only people who can afford to live there are the young and affluent, or people renting their homes through a Local Council or Housing Association.

It is probably a fair statement that the 'old' Bethnal Green didn't have any real charm. But the 'new' Bethnal Green doesn't have any charm or character, unless you think soulless modern buildings, coffee shops and vegan restaurants generate character.

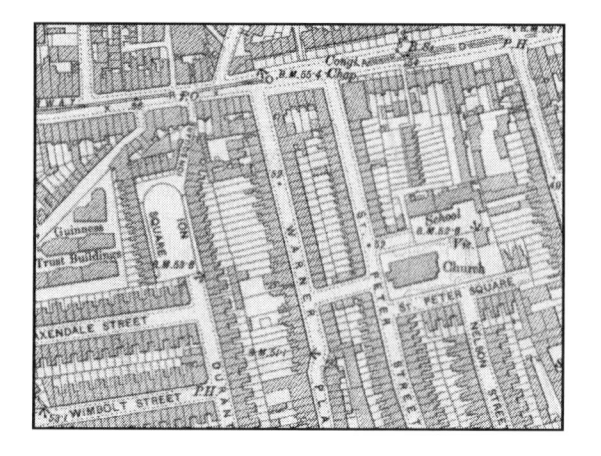

OS Map about 1900

Aerial photograph of the same area now

A 'real' family history

This family history is actually a bit of a cheat. The problem is that it is difficult to know when to stop (researching and writing). There has to be a practical limit if this volume is ever to be finished.

A ploy I have seen other authors use is to cast their net far and wide to find members of the family who are well documented and have had an interesting, exciting or villainous past. The family history in these cases concentrates on these 'stars' to the exclusion of all other family members. However, in the case of the POLAIN family, we seem notably unblessed with well documented, exceptional characters, and to ignore the rest of the family is to deny their existence.

If I was to try to list all my ancestors (male and female) this volume would quickly become unmanageable. At the best of times it can get confusing trying to keep track of who marries who, especially when female POLAINs adopt their husband's surnames on marriage. It can be doubly confusing when widows revert to their maiden names.

For the same reason I have only considered the male POLAINs who were my direct ancestors. As some Victorian families had 10 or 12 children, and complete branches of the family appear to have disappeared entirely over time, it is the only way I could remain sane while trying to piece this tale together.

The saga begins with the birth of Abraham about **1667** in a small village in northern France at a time of great social unrest. But we know little about Abraham, other than he married Barbe (Barbara) and that they had a son called Claude.

So our story really starts in **1701** with the birth of Claude. I then document his descendants that lead directly to me, ignoring all other POLAIN (and POLAINE) families along the way. For

A Brief & Incomplete Family History

those people who have problems sleeping and desire a more detailed list of our descendants, I have included a more detailed family tree inside the back cover (**Appendix J**). For those really sad people with no social life, I have also included details of the reference documents.

I presume Claude was the first POLAIN in the UK, but the records show odd instances of apparently unconnected people with similar names turning up in the UK before Claude. Who these people are, and whether they have any connection to me I have chosen to ignore (unknowns can send you mad if you take them too seriously).

I have been lucky in that I can find documents linking back to Claude (well, at least to Robert). Many other branches of the family just seem to 'disappear' over time. Families with no children: families with no obvious male heir. Or births missing from the records, leading to 'orphans' that I haven't been able to link to the players in our little family saga.

But regardless of any arbitrary decisions on my part on what does and what does not constitute a relation, the fact remains that all I am attempting to do is to use documented facts, and draw lines between the facts to show relationships and context.

The 'facts' are contained in the documents that still exist-the lines connecting the facts are conjecture and subject to misinterpretation and misunderstanding.

Therefore, to get a better understanding of the facts and to draw your own conclusions, you always need to go back to the original documents, which these days are usually to be found on the internet.

Just because I found a Baptism record showing that Alfred William was William James's dad, it doesn't necessarily link Alfred William to the one born in 1799 or to the William James who was married in 1840. It's a lazy assumption made on the fact that the names match, but in a family like ours where names are constantly reused, documents are illegible or inconsistent, a little more academic rigour is required.

And that is the fun of trawling through the old records, like a modern day Hercule Poirot, trying to match locations, dates, names and roles. We are all human and fallible and I am happy to admit I too am human (this admission will come as a surprise to my family) and can make mistakes.

Evolution

I started putting the family history together in the late 1990s when the internet was still taking off and few records were available digitally. Thankfully, things have improved dramatically over the years to the point where most records are available on line. Of course, an Ancestry.com or similar subscription is required to get access to the original documents, but there are still a number of notable hold outs, like the British Museum who have little on line and certainly nothing for free.

The first version of this POLAIN family history was put together in 2016. I was never really happy with it as it seemed jumbled and didn't have a flowing narrative. The revised edition is less jumbled but still lacking in narrative. To supplement the lack of narrative, I have added context to show the world our ancestors lived in. I also took the opportunity to see if I could close out some of the uncertainties by going through the on line records again.

Much to my surprise and delight, Ancestry.com now has the parish records for births and deaths as well as the BMD registers. The parish records contain much more information that lets you accurately 'connect the dots', such as father's name and occupation, sometimes the mother's name, their home addresses, witness's signatures and even if people were illiterate (an X on a wedding register tells its own story).

To date, our little family saga has over 900 names, split into 300 different family groups with a couple of thousand 'facts'. To manage this manually would be a problem but plenty of computer programmes exist to make the task easier. I currently use RootsMagic 8.

The difference with the computer compiled version, compared to this selective and limited printed version, is that all connections, wherever they may lead, are in the computer records. So the POLAINE branch (a spelling variant that seems to have its origin with James Leonard in the 1800s) is covered, as well as many POLAIN/POLAINE connections in Australia (for which our Australian cousins deserve all the credit).

There is no access to official records within the last 100 years. The 1921 census records were released this year and that will be the last census for 20 years (there was no census in 1931 and 1941).

An exercise in futility

If you ever get to the end of this volume, you may realise that this particular branch of the POLAIN family tree ends with me. Anyone who picks up the role of family historian will have to start afresh, from where their back story diverges from mine.

In that respect, this whole book has been a complete waste of my time and effort as I have no children to pass it on to, but it is still something I felt I owed my ancestors.

After all, without them, we wouldn't be here.

Observations

Having poured through these records for some years now, I can't help but come to a number of depressing conclusions.

No matter how much information you can collect, the individuals are reduced to just names. Sometimes these names can be tied to dates and occasionally can be fixed to an address (which has since ceased to exist). No matter how hard we look, regardless of what information we may uncover, we will never be able to see them as living, breathing people.

That is why I have tried to track down the best photographs of the Nichol estate in Bethnal Green– they may not be my ancestors but in these early photographs you can see the faces of the people, of the children, their cloths and the grim living conditions.

I am also convinced that we would struggle to understand the world and the society they lived in. We have grown up in a world where disease is something to be fought and overcome with drugs and medicines. Our ancestors lived in a pre-penicillin world where life was lived on a knife edge and death, infirmity and poverty were just around the corner. Physical hardships were the norm rather than the exception and the living conditions for many of them would have been beyond our comprehension.

I also have a lurking suspicion that if we could travel back in a time machine to meet our ancestors, we probably wouldn't like them very much.

In putting this history together, I have wherever possible tried to put some flesh on the bones of our ancestors by saying more about the world they lived in, so that we can better understand their lives. Hopefully, as time goes on and the research continues, this can be expanded to put the individuals into their full historical context.

I also have a residual feeling (maybe more of a hope really) that there are more answers that we haven't found yet. As a family historian I have lived in hope that tomorrow I would stumble onto an obscure collection of records that will somehow answer all the present unknowns. But no matter how hard we look at the past, we will never fully understand. It is like a giant jigsaw puzzle with pieces missing-but we don't know what is missing as we don't have the picture on the front of the box. Then there are jigsaw pieces that don't seem to fit, but they may not even be from our jigsaw.

As an Engineer and uncomfortable with leaving things uncertain and unresolved, I have found this realisation depressing and constantly have had to resist the urge to hammer the pieces of the jigsaw into place, regardless of how well they actually fit.

Records

I have dipped into the family genealogy as time permitted over the years, and have not been as diligent with my record keeping as I should have. However, I have prepared three binders of documents and information to go with this book.

I mention it in the vague hope that someone in the future will pick up the POLAIN family history and see if there is anything else they can add to it (new records keep coming on line all the time).

The **Record Binder** contains reference documents etc.

It is currently broken into four distinct categories.

BC	Birth Certificates
MC	Marriage Certificates
DC	Death Certificates
OT	Other Things (!)

Parish marriage records can be found on the internet and are accessed using one of the privately owned genealogy companies. Quite why we have to pay private companies to access church and government records is something I have never been able to fathom out. These sites proved useful in providing the names of the husbands for some of the female POLAINs and POLAINEs, however, I didn't make paper copies.

The section that is probably of most interest to the casual reader is the Reference section at the back of the Binder. This contains contemporary maps, newspaper articles etc. that bring a flavour of the lives of our ancestors.

There are two other binders containing original documents, copies of original documents and supporting evidence.

I have imaginatively labeled them **Evidence I** and **Evidence II**.

Evidence I contains copies of the Birth, Deaths and Marriage Registers up to the start of the 20th century. **Evidence II** contains copies of all the census returns between 1841 and 1921 (access to census returns in the last 100 years is not allowed).

There are two particularly interesting books that deal with the social conditions for families living in the Nichol 'slums' during Victorian times.

A Child of the Jago	Arthur Morrison
The Blackest Streets	Sarah Wise

A Brief & Incomplete Family History

Acknowledgements

Text

In putting together this abbreviated family history, I have relied on published source documents, publications and other people's research. I am indebted to them, even if I haven't fully acknowledged their contributions in the text. In particular, Sue Brugnolli has been collecting her family history and as collateral damage has accumulated a lot of information about the POLAIN family. This was useful in confirming the veracity of the information I had collated over the years.

In addition, the descendants of the POLAINs who migrated to Australia have also collected a vast amount of information of the members of the family who left these shores. I have not attempted to document the individual stories of our Australian cousins, and leave this task to others.

Over the years many people have studied the history of their Huguenot ancestors. Due to the unique nature of these names and that their ancestors have married ours, we have been able to drawn on their research. In particularly the Cazaly and Carlier family histories seem intertwined with ours.

The internet has been a wonderful thing as it has made searching, finding and access to historical documents so much easier. Sites run by the **Latter Day Saints**, the **National Archives** at Kew and **Ancestry.com** make the finding and downloading of records quick and easy, which frequently leads to an unwarranted confidence on the part of the author that they understand all the connections and relationships.

Illustrations

I have tried wherever possible to include photographs, drawings and maps to help the reader visualise the world our ancestors would have known. Photographs of modern London are by the author.

The earliest photograph of a family member I have been able to identify is about 1890 but family members have been remarkably shy about having their likenesses recorded for posterity. Looking at the family history, I suspect that cost was a factor (a Kodak for the masses did not really exist before the 1920s). In addition, photographs are frequently discarded when people die and houses are cleared.

As a result, I have had to resort to the internet for illustrations. Many images from the Victorian era appear to have come from private collections, but invariably the sources of the original images were not mentioned. Where the information has been available, I have included an acknowledgement to the photographer or the collection.

A Brief & Incomplete Family History

In a few instances, I have included drawings (or more accurately, engravings) to illustrate items mentioned in the text. In most cases, they come from long gone publications and cannot be attributed. The Holgarth engravings of Gin Lane and Beer Street are the exception and are widely reproduced elsewhere.

Maps, held by Universities and libraries are frequently low resolution, and designed for reading on computer screens. As a result, where I have included an extract from a map I have also included the publisher and date so the original source material can be viewed in high resolution if required.

·······●●●●●●●●●·······

A Brief & Incomplete Family History

PART ONE – THE FAMILY

1 CLAUDE POLAIN (1701-1756)

1.1 Historical Context

A move away from the established Church

From the 15th century, the Catholic church had a dominant position in Europe. Religion and politics were inextricably bound together and led to wars across Europe. Through centuries of successful warfare and strategic marriages, the Holy Roman Empire emerged as monarchs of a large part of Europe.

Roman Catholicism had a hierarchy with the Pope at the apex because he was regarded as the successor to St. Peter, and therefore the undisputed head of the church. God could only be approached through the clergy, the Pope's representatives. As the Bible was in Latin its reading was restricted to a small, educated elite.

In a way, this story of the POLAIN family in the UK started with just two people-Luther and Calvin.

Many people had long been unhappy with the corruption that had crept in to the Church's practices and wanted to return to Biblical teachings. Martin Luther (a German monk) and Jean Calvin (a French theologian based in Switzerland) were determined to reform the church and questioned it's authority.

In 1517 in Germany, Martin Luther tacked 'Ninety-Five Theses' to the door of a Wittenberg church and launched what we now know as the Protestant Reformation. Calvin's ideas on reformation of the Church were published soon after. Followers of these men became known as Protestants and their ideas and beliefs spread across Europe in the 16th Century. Calvin was especially important in France where his followers, drawn primarily from the middle class and skilled artisans, came to be called Huguenots.

They wanted the Bible translated into local languages so that everyone could read it. Their 'churches' were generally small communities, frequently praying together at home. Common Catholic practices, such as the buying of indulgences for the forgiveness of sin, were not tolerated by the Protestants. In particular the Calvinist's didn't believe in a hierarchy within the church, so didn't recognise the authority of the priests and bishops.

The majority of the aristocracy remained loyal to Catholicism. Protestantism appealed mainly to the middle classes and skilled artisans-people who were used to running their own businesses and who resented the intrusion of the Church in their lives.

The Consequences in France

In the late 18th century, France was not a good place to be a Protestant. People's beliefs were quite literally a matter of life or death.

During 1652 and 1698 in France there had been conflict between the Catholics and the Protestants and the persecution of Protestants was tolerated by the authorities if not actively promoted. In 1685 the Edict of Nantes (originally intended to reduce the persecution of Protestants) was repealed and the persecution grew more intense. In 1723, Louise XV re-introduced the old laws originally brought in by his grandfather allowing the persecution to continue. Protestant male worshippers could be sent to the galleys for life, females sentenced to life imprisonment and ministers condemned to death. Children of Protestant marriages were declared illegitimate and could not inherit.

The Protestant communities often met in secret to worship, and few records of their churches survived. After 1685, Protestants were forced to attend Catholic churches and records of births, marriages and deaths would have been recorded in the Catholic church records. However, in the eyes of the Catholic church, Protestants were heretics and couldn't be buried in consecrated ground.

Although leaving the country was forbidden, it is believed that more than 250,000 Protestants left France to seek refuge in more tolerant societies. Many found homes in the Netherlands and America.

The Consequences in England

In England during Henry VIII's reign the Catholic Church and monasteries were dissolved and the Church of England established. The Protestant movement influenced the new Church, but the Calvanists still rejected the appointment of priests and bishops. The more fundamental Protestants were called Puritans in England. This non conformist approach evolved over time into the Congregationalists, the Baptists and the English Presbyterians. (see **Appendix E** for more information about Calvanists)

In keeping with the strong anti-Catholic sentiment of the day, King Charles II flung open the doors of England, offering a refuge to the fleeing Protestants. Thanks to widespread propaganda depicting the persecution inflicted on French Protestants, the refugees arrived to a warm welcome by the English people.

In 1685, James, Duke of York, (a Catholic) became king of England, Ireland and Scotland. James's reign was unpopular with the Protestant majority in Britain. William of Orange, (William III) a Protestant, invaded England in 1689 in what was later known as the 'Glorious Revolution'. He was welcomed by many who feared a revival of Catholicism under James.

Between 40,000 and 50,000 French refugees had made their way to safety in England by 1710. Probably half that number settled in Spitalfields where housing was cheap and the London trade guilds had less economic power.

Timeline

1702   William III died and was succeeded by Anne.
1704   Gibraltar was captured by a combined Dutch and English fleet
1707   The Acts of Union were passed in England and Scotland
1715   First major 'Jacobite' rising begins
1718   British convicts transported to penal colonies overseas
1720   'South Sea Bubble' bursts and triggers a financial panic
1721   Sir Robert Walpole becomes the first prime minister
1727   George I dies and is succeeded by the second Hanoverian king, George II

Famous People

Famous people born between the date of Claude's birth and the birth of his last child, Marie (between 1701-1750). It is unlikely that Claude and his family would have heard of them as the broadsheets were the only form of mass communication.

1709 - 1784   Samuel Johnson
1725 - 1798   Giacomo Casanova
1727 - 1788   Thomas Gainsborough
1728 - 1779   James Cook
1729 - 1796   Catherine the Great
1732 - 1799   George Washington
1736 - 1819   James Watt

Ann (1702-1714)    *George I (1714-1727)*    *George II (1727-1760)*

1.2 Claude's Family

Claude's parents

Claude's parents were **Abraham** Poulain and **Barbe** (Barbara) nee Carlier. Abraham was born about 1667 and was 29 when he married Barbe in the village of Templeux-le-Guerard, near St. Quentin in Picardy in 1696. Claude's father died at the age of 81 in the same village but there is no record of Claude's mother's death.

Over the years the border with modern day Belgium has moved but the village was then, as it is again now, in northern France. Templeux-le-Guerard was one of a number of villages in the St. Quentin / Cambrai area that had been a focus of renewed Protestant activity just a few years before.

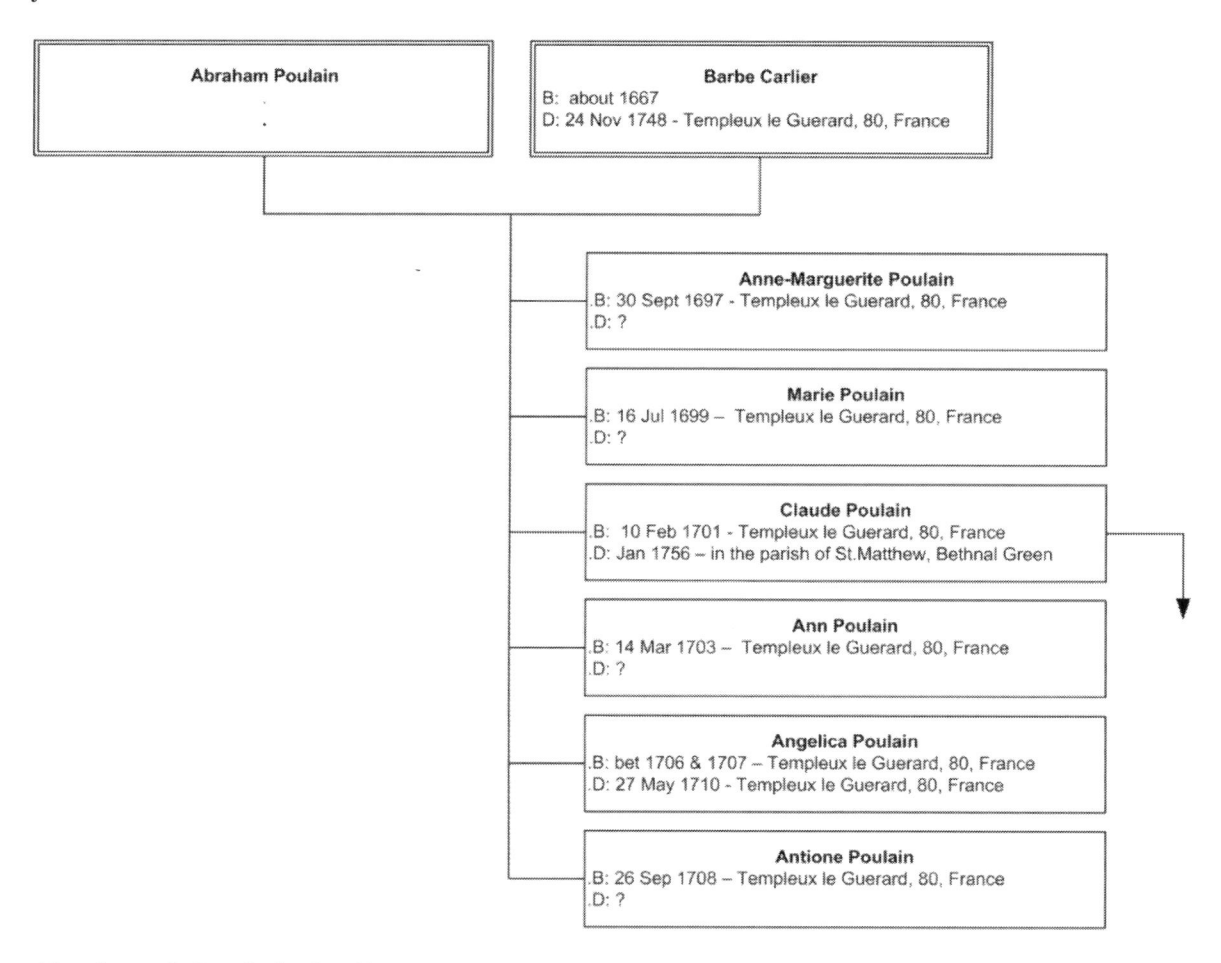

```
Abraham Poulain ─┐
                 │
Barbe Carlier ───┤
B: about 1667    │
D: 24 Nov 1748 - Templeux le Guerard, 80, France
                 │
                 ├── Anne-Marguerite Poulain
                 │   B: 30 Sept 1697 - Templeux le Guerard, 80, France
                 │   D: ?
                 │
                 ├── Marie Poulain
                 │   B: 16 Jul 1699 – Templeux le Guerard, 80, France
                 │   D: ?
                 │
                 ├── Claude Poulain
                 │   B: 10 Feb 1701 - Templeux le Guerard, 80, France
                 │   D: Jan 1756 – in the parish of St. Matthew, Bethnal Green
                 │
                 ├── Ann Poulain
                 │   B: 14 Mar 1703 – Templeux le Guerard, 80, France
                 │   D: ?
                 │
                 ├── Angelica Poulain
                 │   B: bet 1706 & 1707 – Templeux le Guerard, 80, France
                 │   D: 27 May 1710 - Templeux le Guerard, 80, France
                 │
                 └── Antione Poulain
                     B: 26 Sep 1708 – Templeux le Guerard, 80, France
                     D: ?
```

Abraham & Barbe's family

Claude and Barbe

Although we reflect on earlier periods in history (see **Part 2-'Polains' in the Middle Ages**), Claude makes an obvious starting point for this family story for a number of reasons.

Claude was born on 10th February 1701 in the small hamlet of Templeux le Guerard, in what is now called Picardy. Claude had one brother and 4 sisters, although at least one of the sisters died in infancy.

Claude worked as a weaver of Cambric. Cambric, also known as batiste, was one of the finest and most dense kinds of cloth available at the time. It was a lightweight plain-weave cloth, originally from the French commune of Cambrai some 20km away. It was made of linen and was used for shirts, handkerchiefs, ruffs, lace and needlework and was highly prized and expensive. As well as being a skilled artisan, he also learned to read and write. Details about linen and the weaving industry are included in **Appendix C.**

Whilst Claude was still a young man and living in Picardy, there were a number of incidents where Protestants were robbed and beaten by soldiers. The worst incident was in 1717, when soldiers confronted the Protestants in the village and a Madam Dassauville was shot dead, leaving 7 orphans.

Things came to a head when Louise XV came to the throne in 1723 and the persecution of the Protestants became more intense. The measures were aimed at rural Protestants and Templeux-le-Guerard, where the worshippers met in the woods outside the village, would have been a typical target.

First stop-London ....

Some people from the village had already escaped to London. In 1724, Claude, together with Francois Bochard departed via the popular route of Tournai via Dover and they presented their credentials at the French Protestant Church in Threadneedle Street, London on 25th October 1724. It was essential they prove their identity to the Church, to avoid being accused of being Catholic spies. In the following year he married **Catherine Masse** at the same church. (see **Appendix F** for more information about the history of the French Church in London).

There is little information about Catherine except that she came from the adjacent Picardy village of Hesbecourt and that her father's name was Robert. Coincidently, Francois Bochard who travelled to London with Claude, married her sister, Jeanne Masse.

It is probable that Claude and Catherine, with Francois and Jeanne, had travelled from France together as refugees from the persecution, not knowing what they were coming to, only what they were running away from.

In 18th century Europe, travel was not common unless it was needed as part of a job (like soldier or merchant). For a 23 year old to undertake the journey to England, leaving his parents and friends behind, must have been borne out of desperation. Claude had grown up in a small village, miles away from any towns or cities. It is difficult therefore to understand his feelings when he arrived in London- a huge city by the standards of the time.

It is probable that Claude lived initially in the Spitalfields area of London. It was near the church, there were a large number of French Protestant refugees living in the area, and there was an established community of cambric weavers. In 1726 and 1727, Catherine gave birth to two girls, Suzanne and Marie.

Then Scotland ....

Nicholas Dassauville was the uncle of Francois Bochard, who had travelled to London with Claude. He was also the husband of the women shot dead in Templeux in 1717. Dassauville clearly had connections as he was contacted by the **Fisheries and Manufacturers Board of Scotland** to recruit skilled cambric workers to set up a new weaving business in Edinburgh (to compete with a successful business venture in Ireland).

Dassauville recruited the men and their families to travel to Scotland. In 1729, the party took ship from London to Sunderland and from there travelled overland to arrive in Edinburgh in December. In all 9 families moved from London and France to Edinburgh to set up the new enterprise.

Until purpose made premises could be built in Edinburgh, the families lived in rented accommodation in Candle Maker Row (within the Old Town walls and to the east of Gray Friars Church). They were given a weekly subsistence allowance of 10s 6d. (see Map A1 in **Appendix H**)

Workshops and new accommodation were eventually built near Carlton Hill (see Maps A2 to A5 in **Appendix H**)

Life in Edinburgh

For the average Scot, life in Edinburgh's Old Town was miserable.

The rapid expansion of the Old Town within the confines of the city walls committed tens of thousands of citizens to unbearable suffering with little chance of escape. The sky-high tenements, rooms stacked upon rooms in an ungainly fashion, became prisons for rich and poor.

Typically, families resided in a single room and the narrow thoroughfares became a sea of human and animal excrement. Scavengers, paid by the council, swept the streets each evening, removing the filth and depositing it beyond the walls. However, rain often washed it into Nor' Loch, the swamp that bordered one side of Castle Rock and the only source of water for many of the Old Town's residents.

During the daytime, the streets were packed with market stalls of fishmongers, butchers, bakers, candle-makers, weavers and other craftsman. The bloodletting of carcasses and the degutting of fish took place on the streets, with the bodily fluids pooling beneath. But the Old Town was a vibrant and noisy place, dominated by the sounds of tradesman selling their merchandise, animals freely milling around, residents laughing, calling and chatting, and crowds jeering at the sight of miscreants being punished, or hanged, at the Mercat.

Each evening, at ten o'clock, the sound of a drum would instruct residents to retire to their tenements, with the gates to the closes locked overnight.

It was fortunate the 5 acres of land allocated to the Cambric makers to build their workshops was outside the Old Town walls, at the junction of the road to Leith and between Carlton Hill and Broughton. This area was sparsely populated and away from the noise, filth and congestion of the Old Town.

The new building contained 13 units and each family had a vault for weaving and a garret for storing yarn, as well as domestic accommodation consisting of a bedroom and a kitchen. Although basic, it appears each 'house' was 28ft. wide and also provided accommodation for apprentices. When complete the complex would also have a dedicated coalhouse and bake house.

We know exactly where the building was as it is clearly shown on contemporary maps and marked as 'Pickardy'. Even after the 'New Town' was constructed in the 1800s, there was still a 'Piccardy Place' at the same location. Maps of the area are included in the **Appendix H.**

Part of the agreement with the **Fisheries and Manufacturers Board** was that the men would be able to trade in their own right, in addition to providing product for the commune. To facilitate this, all the male immigrants from Picardy were made Burgesses and Guild Brethren of the City of Edinburgh in 1730.

In the same year Claude took on local men, Hugh Brown, John Wallace, Alex Thorburn and James Charlet, as apprentices. The master/apprentice relationships apparently hit bumpy patches over the years, with a number of minor disputes being recorded.

By all accounts, the French weavers were treated well in Scotland, with additional pay (to cover the shortfall in fabric sales in the early years) and to cover their medical costs. However, the enterprise seemed to stumble from crisis to crisis and over the years a number of the original inhabitants moved away.

Family life continued during these business upheavals, and Claude and Catherine had 2 more sons and 5 daughters while living in Edinburgh. Some of the babies did not survive and were buried in the Calton Hill Burial Ground (part of it still survives).

We know that Claude could write, but church records are written by the priests who write down what they think they hear, so consistency in the spelling of family names in the 18th century is the exception rather than the rule. Certainly, when the birth or death of Claude's children was recorded in Scotland, a variety of names appear in the registers. This was probably due to Claude's strong regional accent and that his principal language (maybe his only language) was Picard, a version of Old French.

Scotland had a variety of languages that were either Celtic or Germanic. In southern Scotland until the 1700s, Scottish would have been spoken, but after that time Scottish English became more common. In addition, there were a large number of dialects and strong accents so it is a reasonable assumption that Old French speaking Claude (if not his family) would have struggled to communicate.

Although most supporters of the Jacobites in Scotland were from the Highland clans, there was also support from (Catholic) France. There were repeated reports of planned French invasions to support the Jacobites, so it is quite possible that Claude and his family had been viewed with caution if not outright suspicion by some of the people in Edinburgh.

The original enterprise in Edinburgh eventually expanded under new management and with replacement weavers it developed to become 'The British Linen Company', a hugely successful manufacturer of the time.

And back to London ....

In 1748, Claude moved his now considerably larger family back to London. He again presented his credentials to the French Church in Threadneedle Street on Christmas Day to re-establish his position within the congregation. The presentation of credentials was an essential part of life for the French protestants as they lived in fear of French spies infiltrating the church and reporting back to the authorities in Paris. His eldest son Absalom, who was just 16 at the time, stayed in Scotland for a further 8 years before returning to London. Claude's daughter Marie (recorder as Marian Pillanes from pickarde) stayed on in Scotland, working as a spinner in the commune and died in Edinburgh in 1779 at the age of 52, apparently still a spinster. She was buried at the Carlton Hill Burial Ground with her brothers and sisters who did not survive.

By 1748, Spitalfields had become crowded with the influx of refugees from the continent. Claude and his family moved to Bethnal Green a few miles away, where a number of Protestant weavers had already become established. At the time, Bethnal Green would have been an expanding and developing village on the outskirts of London. It is likely that when the family moved out to Bethnal Green, they had assimilated into the community as the records in the French Protestant church in central London cease and the first entries in St. Matthew's parish register in Bethnal Green are found.

The area between St Matthews and the Cambridge Road to the east was farmland and generally unpopulated. Apart from some houses around Cock Lane, there was no housing north of Hare Street. Therefore, Claude would probably have lived somewhere near Hare Street, St John Street or Silver Street. By living here they would still have been part of the expanded Huguenot community as far as business and social contacts were concerned (see Map B1 opposite and **Appendix H**)

In 1756, at the age of 55, Claude died and his death is recorded in the parish register of St. Matthews, Bethnal Green. There is no record of Catherine's death, which we presume was sometime after 1750 and before 1757.

Claude's children

We have no records of the marriage or death of Suzanne, Elizabeth, Catherine or Marie. We know that at least 4 of the girls died whilst still infants or small children. The girls were buried in the Calton Hill Old Burial Ground.

We only have records for three of Claude's children who survived him.

- **Absalom** - married Jeanne Cazaly at St. Matthew's in Bethnal Green in 1761 when he was 29. The only record after this date is a payment of Land Tax for the room he was renting in Bethnal Green. At the time he was 48 but the records don't show if his wife was still alive or if there were any children.
- **Robert** - married Esther Pennel at St. Matthew's in Bethnal Green in 1764. The couple had 9 children. It is through Robert we trace the Polain name through the generations to the present branch of the family.
- **Marie Madeline** - (possibly also known as Magdelene) married Gillaume Cazaly after the family returned to London as there doesn't seem to be any record of Gillaume having been in Scotland, or of their marriage in the Scottish parish registers. She bore two children and died shortly after.

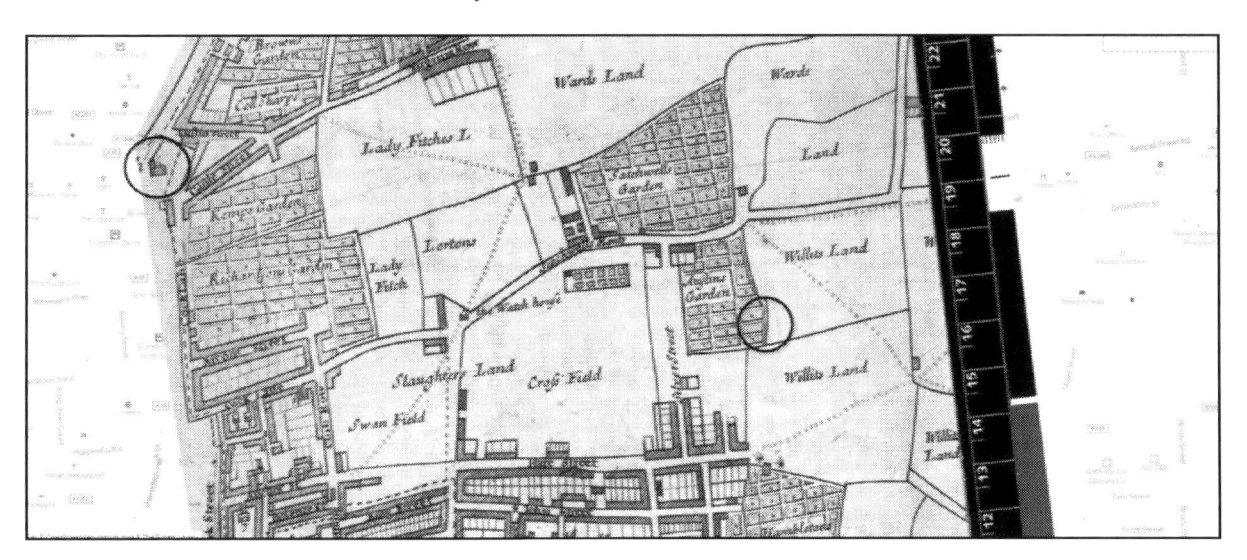

MAP 1 - Part of the 1720 map of the parish of St. Dunstan in the East. St. Dunstan is the oldest church in East London and halfway between London Bridge and the Tower of London. The church was largely destroyed during the Second World War and is now a public garden.

The old St. Leonards church in Shoreditch is in the top left corner of the map (ringed). The present church was built 20 years after this map was published. St Matthew's church will be built on the patch of land between Austin's Garden and the field owned by Willit.

A Brief & Incomplete Family History

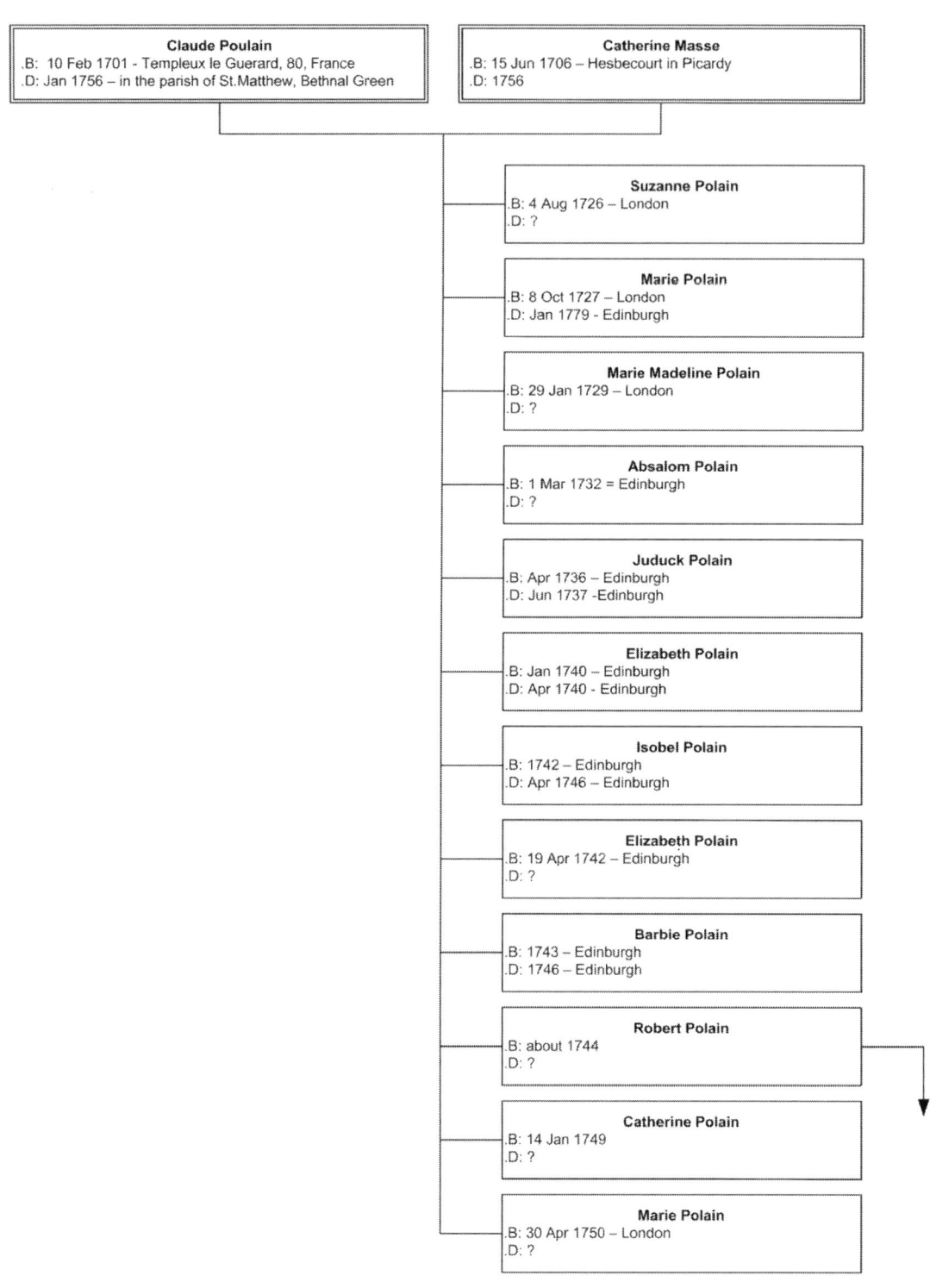

Claude Poulain
.B: 10 Feb 1701 - Templeux le Guerard, 80, France
.D: Jan 1756 – in the parish of St.Matthew, Bethnal Green

Catherine Masse
.B: 15 Jun 1706 – Hesbecourt in Picardy
.D: 1756

- **Suzanne Polain**
  .B: 4 Aug 1726 – London
  .D: ?

- **Marie Polain**
  .B: 8 Oct 1727 – London
  .D: Jan 1779 - Edinburgh

- **Marie Madeline Polain**
  .B: 29 Jan 1729 – London
  .D: ?

- **Absalom Polain**
  .B: 1 Mar 1732 = Edinburgh
  .D: ?

- **Juduck Polain**
  .B: Apr 1736 – Edinburgh
  .D: Jun 1737 - Edinburgh

- **Elizabeth Polain**
  .B: Jan 1740 – Edinburgh
  .D: Apr 1740 - Edinburgh

- **Isobel Polain**
  .B: 1742 – Edinburgh
  .D: Apr 1746 – Edinburgh

- **Elizabeth Polain**
  .B: 19 Apr 1742 – Edinburgh
  .D: ?

- **Barbie Polain**
  .B: 1743 – Edinburgh
  .D: 1746 – Edinburgh

- **Robert Polain**
  .B: about 1744
  .D: ?

- **Catherine Polain**
  .B: 14 Jan 1749
  .D: ?

- **Marie Polain**
  .B: 30 Apr 1750 – London
  .D: ?

Claude's family

1.3 Bits of the Jigsaw

Puzzles and explanations

The life of Claude and his family is well documented because the records of the weaving enterprise in Scotland are extensive, detailed and still exist. In addition, the parish registers give enough clues to marriages and births to help us fill in some of the gaps.

Some records of the Protestants in Picardy have survived. Copies from the internet, in French and without explanation, are included in the Records Binder, Reference **OT113**. There is a phrase that crops up regularly, and that is 'buried in the garden'. I always assumed that this was some sort of euphemism, but more recently I have understood it to be a factual statement. It appears that as Protestants were regarded as heretics by the Catholic Church, they couldn't be buried in consecrated ground. Therefore they were, quite literally, buried in the garden when they died.

The "Records Binder" contains a summary of the evidence by Dr Springall of the Huguenot Society in London, dated 2001. (see reference **OT109**). There is also a copy of an article from the Proceedings of the Huguenot Society, that looks at the Huguenot community in Scotland, specifically looking at the role of the weavers of Picardy (see reference **OT110**).

Although there is no record of Robert being born in Edinburgh, this could be explained by the fact that the local Protestant church records have all been lost. However, the absence of this critical link between Claude and the subsequent generations does pose some problems for the serious and conscientious genealogist-of which I am not one. The only evidence we have that Robert was Claude's son was the petition to the French Hospital by his great-grand daughter as it was necessary to prove her French Protestant heritage to be eligible to be accepted into the Hospital. See Records Binder **OT114** for a transcription of Madelaine's application to the French Hospital, stating her links to her father Robert, and her grandfather, Claude.

Two of Claude's daughters were named "Elizabeth" but this can be explained as the first child died before the age of 1 and the sister who was born a few years later took the name. However, three of Claude's daughters appear to have "Marie" as their first name and the same explanation of infant mortality cannot be applied.

Claude's Will

Claude's last will and testament survived. It says:

> *"I give all that which is in my house, moveable and immovable and the interest of what I have belonging to me at the Bank to my wife during her life. The capital shall be for my children they shall share altogether alike without any distinction. My wife Catherine Polain shall be Executor of my will."*

The surviving record of the will is a translation from the original in French. A copy of it is included in the "Records Binder" under the reference **OT109**.

It is interesting that even after 30 years in England, his preferred language was still French. Indeed it is quite possible, looking at evidence from modern day London, that he spoke no English at all. It is also interesting to note that he didn't own the house where he lived but had sufficient savings in the bank for his wife to live off the interest.

The fact that Claude's will survived suggests that he was not poor and the fact that his money was in a bank suggests a certain degree of wealth.

In the margin of Claude's will there is a note that gives some helpful information. Apparently, Catherine died after the will was written but left no will of her own and died intestate. Therefore Absalom had to go to the Court to have the estate granted to him as the eldest son.

Spellings

Up to this point, the spelling of the family name had been inconsistent on the surviving records but the will written by Claude and the Petition, written by Absalom, both used the current spelling of POLAIN.

It is interesting that the French web sites list 'POLAIN' as a characteristically Protestant family name in France, rather than any of the 'misspelled' variants. Perhaps it was only the priests in Scotland recording the births, deaths and marriages that had any problem with the spelling.

It is also interesting to see the name 'POLAIN' cropped up in Medieval France at the end of the 13th century. I give more details and the context in **Part 2**. Of course, it is highly speculative to think there is any connection between them and our ancestors, but speculating is fun, and the story of the feud between Waroux and Awans is fascinating.

Some years later, a variation would creep into the spelling of the family name, when an 'e' was inadvertently added to the end of the name. That error appears to have stuck with that branch of the family until the current time.

Claude's birthplace today

Claude and Catherine came from the villages of Templeux-le-Guerard and Hesbecourt, in Picardy. There are still villages with the same name only a few kilometres apart but whether they are actually in the same places as the original villages we cannot know. However, the villages are tiny and Hesbecourt appears to be no more than a few farm buildings. Templeux-le-Guerard consists of small private houses along the roadside where two roads meet.

The area doesn't appear to be heavily populated or wealthy. The impression of the countryside is of large, open, rolling fields with villages few and far between. We can assume the landscape is the result of hundreds of years intensive cultivation.

Templeux-le-Guerard in 2006

Claude's time was before the Industrial Revolution and the mass movement of people from rural areas to urban conurbations. I presume that in Claude's time the area would have been filled with small family farms and small holdings.

The villages are on the edge of the area that was affected by the battle of the Somme (there is a small WW1 graveyard in Templeux-le-Guerard) and there are no buildings in the villages that appear to pre-date the war, except a small Protestant church.

18th century London

These engravings by Hogarth (overleaf) give a vivid picture of life in the city in 1751. Hogarth portrays the inhabitants of Beer Street as happy and healthy, nourished by the native English ale, and those who live in Gin Lane as destroyed by their addiction to the foreign spirit of gin. "**Gin Lane**" shows scenes of infanticide, starvation, madness, decay and suicide, while "**Beer Street**" depicts industry, health, bonhomie and thriving commerce.

> *From Wikipedia*
>
> *The gin crisis was severe. From 1689 onward the English government encouraged the industry of distilling, as it helped prop up grain prices, which were then low, and increase trade, particularly with England's colonial possessions. Imports of French wine and spirits were banned to encourage the industry at home.*
>
> *In the heyday of the industry there was no quality control whatsoever; gin was frequently mixed with turpentine, and licences for distilling required only the application. When it became apparent that copious gin consumption was causing social problems, efforts were made to control the production of the spirit. The Gin Act 1736 imposed high taxes on sales of gin, forbade the sale of the spirit in quantities of less than two gallons and required an annual payment of £50 for a retail licence. This had little effect beyond increasing smuggling and driving the distilling trade underground.*
>
> *The prohibitive duty was gradually reduced and finally abolished in 1743. Francis Place later wrote that enjoyments for the poor of this time were limited: They often had only two: "...sexual intercourse and drinking," and that "...drunkenness is by far the most desired..." as it was cheaper and its effects more enduring.*
>
> *By 1750 over a quarter of all residences in St Giles parish in London (north of Covent Garden) were gin shops, and most of these also operated as receivers of stolen goods and coordinating spots for prostitution.*

A Brief & Incomplete Family History

Gin Lane

A Brief & Incomplete Family History

Beer Street

2 ROBERT POLAIN (1744-????)

2.1 Historical Context

Life in the 18th Century

The 18th century was a period of rapid growth for London, the early stirrings of the Industrial Revolution, and London's role at the centre of the evolving British Empire. By 1715, London's population reached an estimated 630,000 people, approximately 750,000 people by 1760 and 1 million by the end of the century.

London's growth in the 18th century was marked above all by the westward shift of the population away from the City of London. Westminster was intensively developed, with new districts like Mayfair housing Britain's wealthiest aristocratic families. By 1738 nearly the whole space between Piccadilly and Oxford Street was covered with buildings as far as Park Lane. Rural villages outside of London proper also grew in population and were gradually incorporated into the urban fabric: areas like Bethnal Green and Shadwell to the east, or Paddington and St Pancras to the northwest.

With the completion of Westminster Bridge in 1750, London gained a much needed second overland crossing into the South Bank. In 1761 the seven ancient gates enclosing the City of London were removed to improve the circulation of traffic, as was the dense warren of housing on London Bridge which was a perennial fire hazard.

Landmark legislation included the Westminster Paving Act of 1765, which required streets be equipped with pavements, drainage, and lighting. The success of the legislation inspired the London Paving and Lighting Act of 1766, which extended the same provisions across the whole city and required that houses be numbered and streets and pavements be cleansed and swept regularly. Street lighting was more extensive than in any other city in Europe, something which amazed foreign visitors to the capital in the late 18th century.

A phenomenon of 18th-century London was the coffee house, which became a popular place to debate ideas. Growing literacy and the development of the printing press meant that news became widely available. Fleet Street became the centre of the embryonic British press during the century.

The Bow Street Runners were established in 1749 as a professional police force. Penalties for crime were harsh, with the death penalty being applied for fairly minor crimes. Public hangings were common in London, and were popular public events.

In 1780, London was rocked by the Gordon Riots, an uprising by Protestants against Roman Catholic emancipation led by Lord George Gordon. Severe damage was caused to Catholic churches and homes, and 285 rioters were killed.

For every 1,000 children born in early-18th-century London, almost 500 died before they were 2 years old, generally due to malnutrition, bad water, dirty food, and poor hygiene.

Poor craftsmen and labourers lived in just two or three rooms, and the poorest families lived in just one room with very simple and plain furniture. It was a difficult life for poor people: There was no government assistance for the unemployed, and many had trouble finding their next meal or a warm place to sleep.

Poor people ate rather plain and monotonous diets made up primarily of bread and potatoes; meat was an uncommon luxury.

Schools were not compulsory, but many upper-class boys attended school, and some girls from well-off families did, too. Girls were educated more in "accomplishments" like embroidery and music than in academic subjects.

Some "charity schools" started to provide an education to lower-class children. Orphans roamed the streets; because they didn't attend school, they had little chance of improving their situation.

Timelines

1740s

- Sir Robert Walpole resigns as prime minister
- Handel's 'Messiah' gets its first performance, in Dublin
- 'Rule, Britannia' first performed
- George II becomes the last British monarch to lead his army into battle
- 'Bonnie Prince Charlie' lands in Scotland to claim the British throne
- Jacobites are defeated at Culloden, the last battle on British soil

1750s

- Scottish landlords start evicting tenants in the Highland Clearances
- A study shows of the 2339 children admitted into London work houses, only 168 remain alive after five years.
- The Louvre Museum in Paris opens.
- To combat the rampant alcoholism, a gin tax is levied.
- Britain joins Prussia and attacks France, finally defeating her in 1759.
- The British under Wolfe defeat the French near Quebec City. Britain takes possession of New France (Canada) and now controls about half of North America.

1760s

- George III has assumed the throne and desires a more powerful monarchy. He stacks the Parliament in his favour, but meets with public disapproval.
- Canals begin to improve transportation.
- HMS Victory launched in Chatham.
- Factories spring up as improved iron smelting allows factories nearer coal fields.
- In 1770 Captain Cook claims Australia for Britain, landing in Botany Bay.

1770s

- Slavery is ended in Britain, but continues in her colonies.
- War of American Independence is begun.
- Captain James Cook becomes first European to cross the Antarctic Circle.
- The steam engine to power a pump for mining is made in 1775, thus beginning the Industrial Revolution. Before this time, most machines that existed were powered by water, wind and people in small factories or at home "cottage industries".

Famous People

Famous people born between the date of Robert's birth and the birth of his last child, William (between 1744-1778).

1754 – 1817	Captain Bligh
1755 – 1824	Louis XVIII
1756 - 1791	Wolfgang Mozart
1758 - 1805	Horatio Nelson
1759 – 1796	Robert Burns
1761 - 1850	Marie Tussaud
1769 – 1852	1st Duke of York
1769 – 1821	Napoleon Bonaparte
1770 - 1827	Ludwig van Beethoven
1770 – 1850	Wordsworth
1771 - 1833	Richard Trevithick
1775 - 1851	JM Turner

George III (1760-1820)

A Brief & Incomplete Family History

2.2 Robert's Family

Robert and Ester

Because of the records kept at St Matthew's Church in Bethnal Green, we know of Robert and the birth dates of his family but little else.

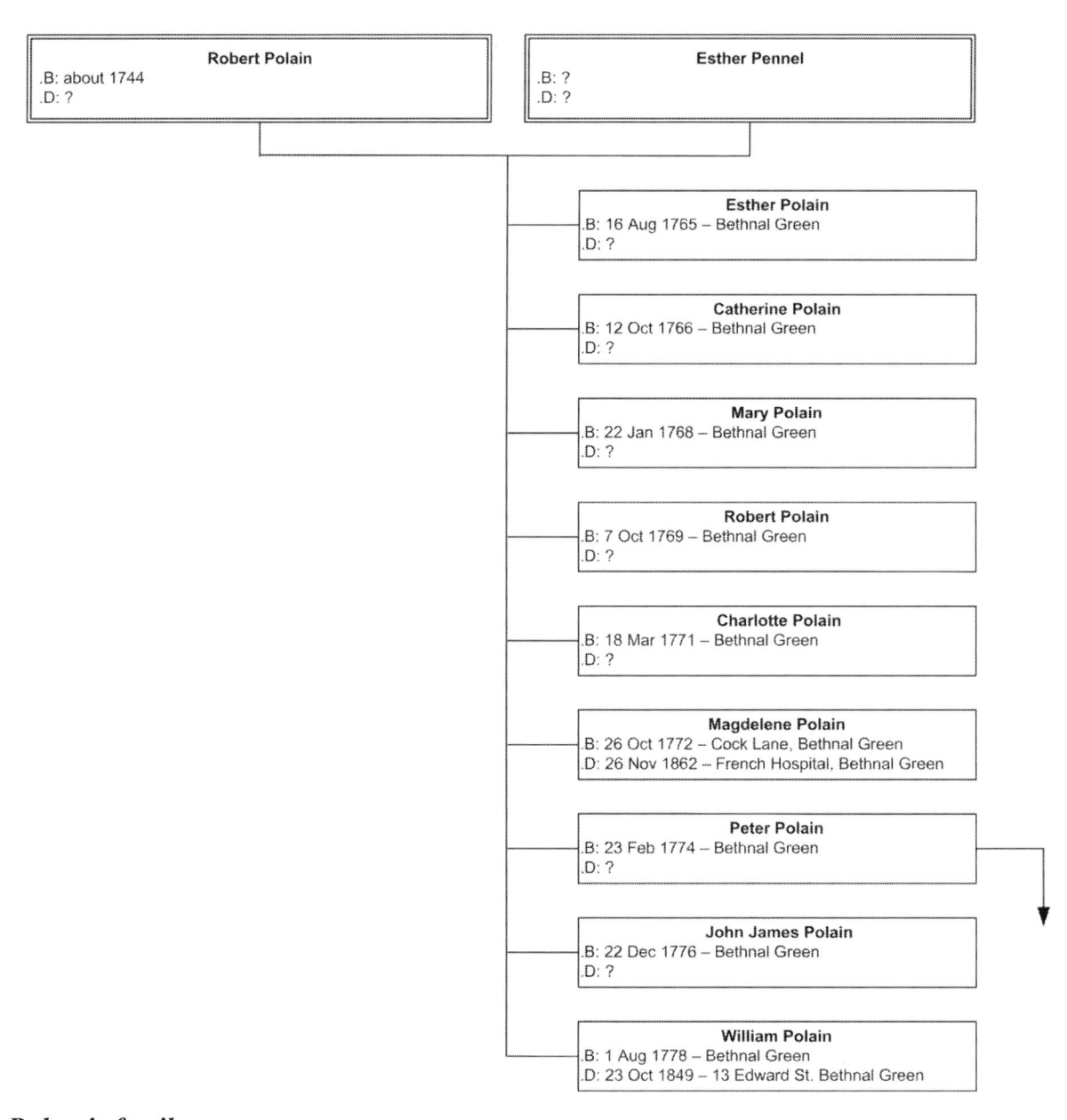

Robert Polain
- .B: about 1744
- .D: ?

Esther Pennel
- .B: ?
- .D: ?

Children:

Esther Polain
- .B: 16 Aug 1765 – Bethnal Green
- .D: ?

Catherine Polain
- .B: 12 Oct 1766 – Bethnal Green
- .D: ?

Mary Polain
- .B: 22 Jan 1768 – Bethnal Green
- .D: ?

Robert Polain
- .B: 7 Oct 1769 – Bethnal Green
- .D: ?

Charlotte Polain
- .B: 18 Mar 1771 – Bethnal Green
- .D: ?

Magdelene Polain
- .B: 26 Oct 1772 – Cock Lane, Bethnal Green
- .D: 26 Nov 1862 – French Hospital, Bethnal Green

Peter Polain
- .B: 23 Feb 1774 – Bethnal Green
- .D: ?

John James Polain
- .B: 22 Dec 1776 – Bethnal Green
- .D: ?

William Polain
- .B: 1 Aug 1778 – Bethnal Green
- .D: 23 Oct 1849 – 13 Edward St. Bethnal Green

Robert's family

Whilst it is probable that Robert was born whilst his parents lived in Edinburgh, the first clear evidence we have of his existence is his marriage to Esther on 22 September 1764 at St Matthews in Bethnal Green. Her maiden name is unclear in the church records but could be 'Pennel'.

Robert's Children

Over the next 13 years, Robert and Esther had a total of 9 children; 5 girls and 4 boys. The last child was born in 1778, and after this date the records cease. It is not possible to determine if this was because of the death of either Robert or Esther or if Esther's child bearing days had naturally come to an end.

- **Esther**, was born in 1765

- **Catherine** was born in 1766

- **Mary** was born in 1768

- **Robert**, was born in 1769

- **Charlotte** was born in 1771

- **John James** who was born in 1776.

- **Magdelane** was born in 1772 and worked for at least some of her life as a domestic servant. Cock Lane (later known as Boundary Street near Shoreditch) is given as her birthplace but the French Hospital records show her as living at 7 James Street. At some point, probably when she could no longer work to support herself, she applied to be admitted to the French Hospital in Bethnal Green. This was a charitable institution that looked after elderly and infirm persons, as long as they could demonstrate they were of French Protestant descent (See **Appendix D**).

    The records of the French Hospital show she used her maiden name but this doesn't mean that she had remained unmarried, as it was common for widows to revert to their maiden name when their husbands died.

    For the census in 1862, she is shown as a resident at the French Hospital and having an age of 89. She died the following year and was buried in Victoria Park Cemetery.

- **William**, the youngest child in Robert and Esther's family that we know of, was born in August 1778. He married Elizabeth Shoard at Islington Parish Church in 1802. William and Elizabeth had 4 children, including 3 girls.

    o   **Charlotte** (born 1803)

    o   **Catherine** (born 1806)

- - **Esther** (born 1810)

  - **William** (born in 1804). He married Martha Elizabeth Holley in 1831 at Greyfriars, Newgate. They had two children but Martha, who was slightly older than William, died in 1852. William survived her by thirty years, eventually dying in Islington in 1881.

- **Peter Polain** was born in February 1774 and married Mary Ann Billington at the age of 29.

  The story of his family is contained in the next section as he was a direct ancestor of the author.

2.3 Bits of the Jigsaw

Robert, the son of Claude?

Amongst the Polain family genealogists (yes, there are some!) the link between Robert and Claude is tenuous as there is no documentary evidence linking them. However, a strong link was inadvertently provided some 100 years later when Madelaine Polain applied to enter the French Hospital. The French Hospital had firm rules about the applicants being direct descendants of the original Huguenot immigrants. To prove her case she cites Claude as being her direct ancestor. It is unlikely she would have known anything of Claude other than from the verbal accounts passed down within the family.

See Record Binder reference **OT114** for Madelaine's application, mentioning Robert and Claude.

Church Records

Records at the church are good for Christenings (they were often the only record that someone existed) but less so for Weddings and nonexistent for Deaths (sometimes there were records of burials). Partly, this is a consequence of the Church's records showing the dates of services and ceremonies, rather than the actual dates of birth and death. In this respect, it doesn't mean that members of the family were not buried at the church, only that there was no ceremony associated with the burial and therefore no record.

Church Attendance

As St Matthew's was used to record the births of Robert's children, we can assume he drifted away from the French Reform Church towards the Anglican Church. At this time there were a huge number of churches and meeting houses in Bethnal Green, catering for everyone from Baptists to Methodists and Unitarians and Quakers.

Addresses and Trades

Before the 1841 census we have no information on the family's addresses. Trades were not listed until the 1851 census.

The Births, Deaths and Marriage Registers for England and Wales did not start until 1837. Until then we only have church records and these are usually the date of the church activity (i.e. the date of christening rather than date of birth; the date of burial, not the date of death)

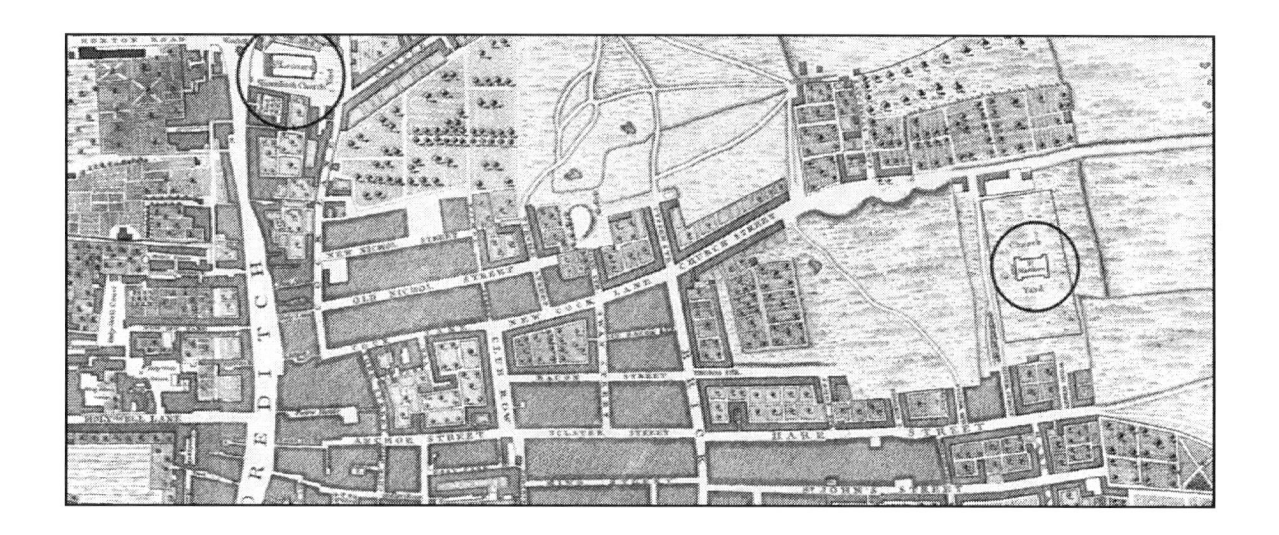

MAP 2 - 1746 map showing west Bethnal Green. The two churches of St. Leonard (top left) and St. Matthews (right) have now been built and are circled.

The area around Nichol Street has been built up since the last map of the area. A 'new' Nichol Street has been built to the north and the original Nichol Street has been renamed 'Old Nichol Street'. Many of the streets in this area will have the name 'Nichol' after the lawyer who bought the land originally in the 17th Century.

There is also new housing in Turvile Street, Club Row, Bacon Street and Sclater Street.

Bethnal Green stretches from Shoreditch in the west to the Cambridge Road in the east. There is a street running nearly parallel to Shoreditch called Boundary Street (previously known as Cock Lane). This was the boundary between the parishes of St Leonards and St Matthews.

(See **Appendix H** for a larger scale version of this map)

3   PETER POLAIN   (1774-????)

3.1   Historical Context

A Changing World

The most notable features of this period were the American and French Revolutions, the rise of Napoleon and the impact and consequences of the Industrial Revolution in Britain.

The American Revolution arose from growing tensions between residents of Great Britain's 13 North American colonies and the colonial government, which represented the British crown. Skirmishes between British troops and colonial militiamen in Lexington and Concord in April 1775 kicked off the armed conflict, and by the following summer, the rebels were waging a full-scale war for their independence.

France entered the American Revolution on the side of the colonists in 1778, turning what had essentially been a civil war into an international conflict. After French assistance helped the Continental Army force the British surrender at Yorktown, Virginia, in 1781, the Americans had effectively won their independence, though fighting would not formally end until 1783.

In France, King Louis XVI tried to raise taxes, which led to protests. On July 14 1789 the Paris mob, hungry due to a lack of food from poor harvests, upset at the conditions of their lives and annoyed with their King and Government, stormed the Bastille fortress (a prison). This turned out to be more symbolic than anything else as only four or five prisoners were found.

In October 1789, King Louis and his family were moved from Versailles to Paris. He tried to flee in 1791, but was stopped and forced to agree to a new form of government. Replacing the power of the King, a 'legislative assembly' governed from October 1791 to September 1792, and was then replaced by the 'National Convention'. The Republic of France was declared, and soon the King was put on trial. The Revolution became more and more radical and violent. King Louis XVI was executed on January 21 1793. In the six weeks that followed some 1,400 people who were considered potential enemies to the Republic were executed in Paris.

Napoleon Bonaparte rapidly rose through the ranks of the military during the French Revolution. After seizing political power in France in a 1799 coup d'état, he crowned himself emperor in 1804.

Shrewd, ambitious and a skilled military strategist, Napoleon successfully waged war against various coalitions of European nations and expanded his empire. However, after a disastrous French invasion of Russia in 1812, Napoleon abdicated the throne two years later and was exiled to the island of Elba. In 1815, he briefly returned to power in his Hundred Days campaign. After a crushing defeat at the Battle of Waterloo, he abdicated once again and was exiled to the remote island of Saint Helena, where he died at 51.

Unlike the American and French Revolutions, the Industrial Revolution had no clearly defined beginning or end. It quickly spread across the world.

An outstanding feature of the Industrial Revolution was the advance in power technology. At the beginning of this period, the major sources of power available to industry were animal power and the power of wind and water. Originally the only exceptions were the steam engines that had been installed for pumping purposes, mainly in coal mines. Steam did not simply replace other sources of power: it transformed them.

James Watt patented a separate condenser in 1769, and from that point onward the steam engine underwent almost continuous improvements for more than a century. Between 1775 and 1800 some 500 engines were built, which despite their high cost were eagerly acquired by the tin-mining industrialists of Cornwall and other power users who badly needed a more economic and reliable source of energy.

The new steam engines were quickly adopted by British textile manufacturers and later applied to large scale grain milling. Many other industries followed in exploring the possibilities of steam power, and it soon became widely used.

Gas lighting was being developed in the UK and France, with Pall Mall having street lighting in 1807. By 1812 The Gas, Light and Coke Company (forerunner of British Gas) had been established and Preston became the first town to have street lighting, fuelled by coal gas. By 1826, the first gas cooker had been designed. By 1827, there were 70,000 street lights in London, but it wasn't until the development of the gas mantle 50 years later that gas had any widespread use in lighting homes.

Timelines

1780s

- By 1783, Great Britain recognizes the new United States of America.
- The slave trade is delivering 100,000 slaves to North America each year.
- Penal colonies are established in Australia. Breech-loading guns replace barrel-loaded muskets.
- The spinning-mule revolutionizes the textile industries but is soon overtaken by the steam-driven loom. High quality cast iron can now be made through a continuous process and becomes prolific.
- Steam improves production in mines, blast furnaces, spinning and weaving factories, paper mills, flour mills and breweries. Coal and iron have taken over from wood and water.
- Education of youth begins in "Sunday Schools", as most youths work during the week.

1790s

- Revolution in France. France declares war on Britain, whose challenges are increased by a revolt in Ireland and mutiny in the British navy. French ports are blockaded.

- Smuggling is rampant. Government responses to internal upheavals include banning trade unions, censoring the press, and rounding up subversives.
- An attempt to abolish slavery across the empire fails. Canada is divided into an upper English half, and lower French half.

1800s

- The Industrial Revolution is in full swing. Wages for women and children decline.
- Trade with Europe is inhibited by the wars with France's self-proclaimed Emperor Napoleon.
- The nation becomes the United Kingdom of Great Britain and Ireland.
- Emigration begins as poor people seek escape from the changing industrial landscape.
- Slave trade is ended, and a steam locomotive appears at a London "steam circus" for the first time.
- Battle of Trafalgar and Nelson's death

1810s

- Economic depression comes on the heels of two foreign wars. The Napoleonic wars end with final British victory over France at Waterloo, and the war with the United States is a draw.
- George IV became regent as ailing King George III was too ill to govern.
- The first steam ship crosses the Atlantic in 26 days. Conventional sailing ships took at least 60 days.

Famous People

1781 – 1848	George Stevenson
1791 – 1867	Michael Faraday
1792 – 1822	Percy Shelley
1795 – 1821	John Keats
1797 – 1828	Franz Schubert
1802 – 1889	John Cadbury
1805 – 1875	Has Christian Anderson
1806 – 1859	Isambard Kingdom Brunel
1809 – 1882	Charles Darwin
1809 – 1865	Abraham Lincoln

George IV (1810 – 1830)

3.2 Peter's Family

Peter and Mary

Peter was born on 23rd February 1774 and baptised on the 9th March at St. Matthews, Bethnal Green.

He was married to Mary Ann Billington at St. Marys Church, Islington. Peter was 29. We have no information on Mary's age, parents or place of birth.

Peter's Children

Clearly, the family had got off to a flying start as their first daughter was born just 3 months after the wedding. Peter and Mary would go on to have a further 8 children (that we know of) over the next 20 years. Only 2 were girls.

- **Sarah Elizabeth** was born 31st May 1804. She married George Swan on 27th May 1822 at St. Lukes Church, Old Street. We have no record of her in the census records up to and including 1861 or of her death. However, there is a death registered of a "Sarah Eliza Swan" who died in Bethnal Green in 1858, although we cannot be confident it was Peter and Mary's daughter as no age is given in the Register index.

- **Robert Alexander** was born 3rd June 1807 and baptised on the 12th June the following year at St. Matthews, Bethnal Green. Robert married Charlotte Overy on 16th July 1827 at St. Leonard's, Shoreditch. Robert was 20 years old when he married. They had 6 children (3 boys, 3 girls) between 1828 and 1839.

    - **Charlotte Mary** was born about 1828 and married William Deighton, who was the same age. They had one child, a girl named after her mother, born in 1850.

    - **Mary Ann** was born about 1830 but we have no further records for her.

    - **John** was born 2 years later but we have no further records for him

    - **Sarah Elizabeth** was born about 1834. She married Thomas Richard Freeman on 21st June 1857 at St. Matthew's, Bethnal Green.

    - **Robert Joseph** was born about 1836 but died within 3 years

    - **Peter** was born in 1839 and married Hannah Butler in July 1863. Their first child was born in 1865 and they went on to have 6 more children in the next 24 years.

    Charlotte died in Hackney in 1869 whilst Robert died in Bethnal Green in 1873, at the age of 66.

A Brief & Incomplete Family History

- **Peter Thomas** was born on 6th October 1812 (as Napoleon Bonaparte's army was retreating from Moscow). He married Sarah Louise, who was 11 years younger than him, and they had two boys. Sarah died in 1871 and Peter died in 1877, both in Bethnal Green.

- **John William** was baptised on 15th May 1816 at St. Leonard's, Shoreditch. He married Elizabeth Frankis in 1841 at St. Matthew's. For the 1841 and the 1851 census, he listed his occupation as 'Cooper' i.e. making barrels for wine. In 1841 he and Elizabeth shared a house with 3 other people in Wolverley Street, just off Bethnal Green Road and Canrobert Street. Two of the other residents of Wolverley Street were identified as weavers.

  Before 1845, the family moved to Westminster and their addresses are recorded in the census returns for 1871 to 1891. John and Elizabeth had 8 children over the following 16 years, 6 of them boys.

  - **John William** was born on 27 December 1841.

  - **Emily** was born in 1843. She married Job Mortimer in 1873 when she was 30 and Job was 66. He died the following year and Emily died in 1876. Job's occupation is listed as 'Waiter' so we can presume that money wasn't the motive for the marriage.

  - **Alfred George** was born on 23rd April 1845. He married Harriet Hurrel about 1876 and died in 1901

  - **Henry Peter** was born in 1847 but we have no further information on his life or death.

  - **Charles** was born in August 1849 and was baptised the following December. He was recorded in the census of 1871 and 1881 as a "Porter" and "Carman"(?) and lived at home with his mother until his death in 1890.

  - **Elizabeth** was born in 1851 and died at the age of 26, never having been married.

  - **William James** was born in 1853 and married Mary Ann Beedell in 1885. In the census returns his occupation was listed variously as *'Tailor & Shoemaker'*, *'Boot and Shoe Maker'* and *'Shoeblack'*. One wonders if this reflects a decline in William's employment status. He died on 1938 at the age of 85.

  - **Frederick Herbert** was born in 1857 in Westminster. His wife was Sarah Amelia White, and they had 5 children. The youngest boy died whilst still an infant. His older brother, Albert Edward was a brush maker who died during the Battle of the Somme. The body was never recovered and his death is recorded on the memorial at Thiepval.

  John died in June 1867 whilst his wife lived on to the age of 83. The 1891 census shows her living with her son William at 51, Beak Street, Westminster. She died about 1901

- **James William** was born in 1817 but we have no other information

- **James Leonard** spelt his name **POLAINE** and so have his descendents. He was born in 1820 and married Hannah Hopkins in 1840. James and Hannah had 12 children (5 girls).

    - **Hannah** and **Sarah** were born in 1841 and 1843 respectively but we have no further records of their lives or deaths.

    - **John James** was born in 1845. He married Sophia Dellow in 1866 at St. Matthew's. They had 3 boys and 1 girl between 1867 and 1882. John died in 1891. He was a boot maker.

    - **James Leonard** (junior) was born in 1846, He married Harriet in 1868 and they had 3 boys and 2 girls between 1868 and 1878. James died in 1884.

    - **William** died in 1853, at the age of 2.

    - **Emma** and **Matilda** were born in 1853 and 1857 respectively but we have no further records of their lives or deaths.

    - **Peter** was born in 1856 and married Maria. There is no record of any children. Peter died in 1933.

    - **William George** was born in 1858 in Mile End New Town He married Jane about 1876 and had two girls. There is no record of his death that we can trace.

    - **Albert Edward** was born in 1861 but died before he was a year old.

    - **Caroline** was born in 1863 but died before she was a year old.

    - **Daniel George** was born in 1865. We have no records of his life or death.

- **Mary Ann** was born in 1824 but we have no records of her life, marriage or death.

- **George Peter** was born in April 1809 and married Elizabeth Dabbs at the age of 22.

The story of George and Elizabeth's family is contained in the next section as he was a direct ancestor of the author.

A Brief & Incomplete Family History

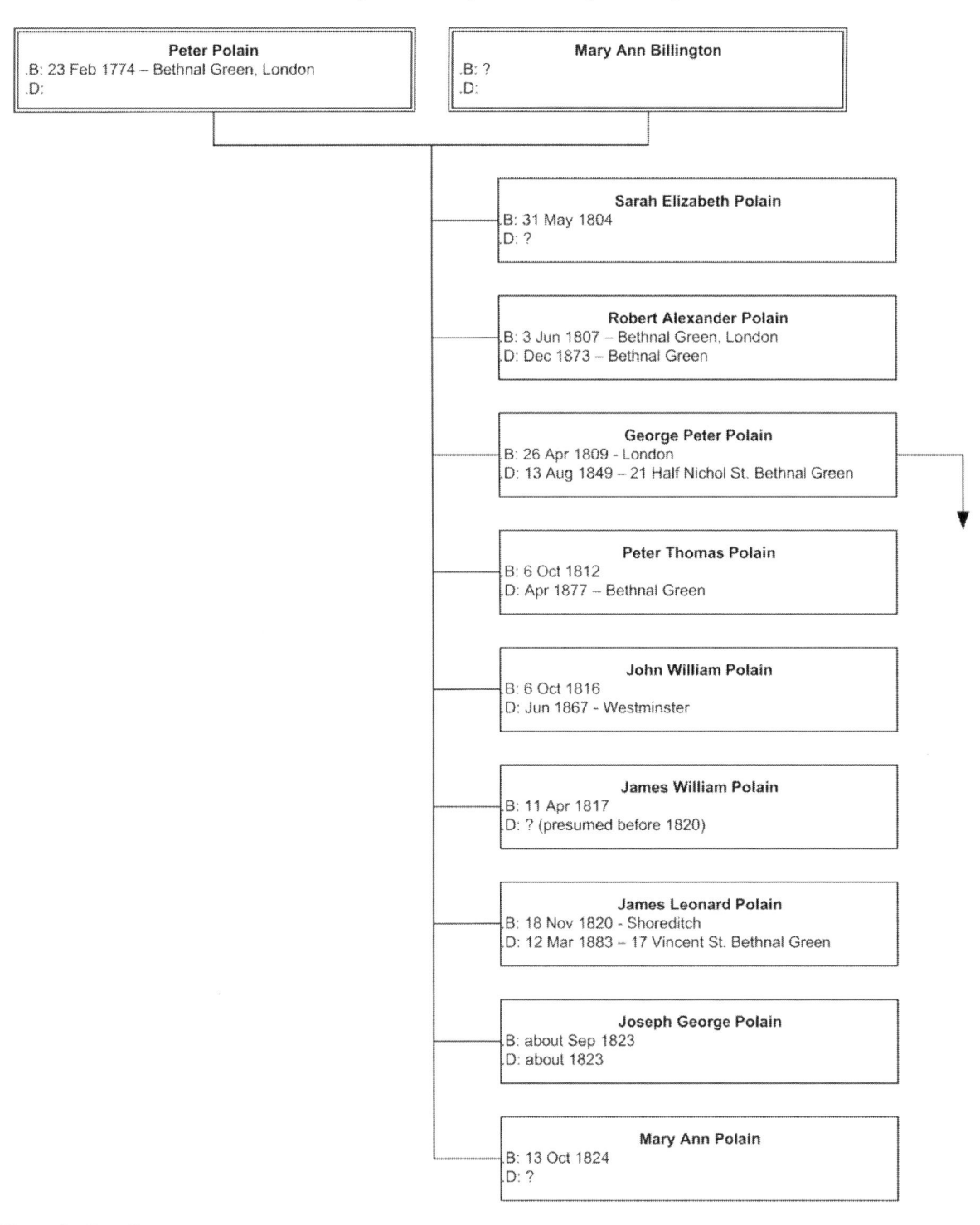

Peter Polain
B: 23 Feb 1774 – Bethnal Green, London
D:

Mary Ann Billington
B: ?
D:

Sarah Elizabeth Polain
B: 31 May 1804
D: ?

Robert Alexander Polain
B: 3 Jun 1807 – Bethnal Green, London
D: Dec 1873 – Bethnal Green

George Peter Polain
B: 26 Apr 1809 - London
D: 13 Aug 1849 – 21 Half Nichol St. Bethnal Green

Peter Thomas Polain
B: 6 Oct 1812
D: Apr 1877 – Bethnal Green

John William Polain
B: 6 Oct 1816
D: Jun 1867 - Westminster

James William Polain
B: 11 Apr 1817
D: ? (presumed before 1820)

James Leonard Polain
B: 18 Nov 1820 - Shoreditch
D: 12 Mar 1883 – 17 Vincent St. Bethnal Green

Joseph George Polain
B: about Sep 1823
D: about 1823

Mary Ann Polain
B: 13 Oct 1824
D: ?

Peter's family

3.3 Bits of the Jigsaw

Food for the masses

Meat
Large quantities of meat had to be transported from the farms to the cities and the quality of meat was bound to be coarse and inferior. A doctor in 1788 warned that the odour of meat was such that one should keep it away from their nose while eating it!

Fruit and Vegetables
Only wealthy people had access to fruit. Today people worry about pesticides, but the good old days may never have existed for fruits or vegetables. In eighteenth-century England they were dirty in the first place and vendors sometimes used saliva as a cleanser!

Cheese
Many types of English cheese became available during this time; a minimum of 40 different kinds have been documented.

Sugar
In the 1790s, the typical English individual consumed about four kilograms of sugar each year.

Bread
A key element of bread in eighteenth-century British bread was alum, which is a bleaching ingredient that also makes bread look bigger.

Milk
A general eighteenth-century England rule for milk: if it was not watered, it was probably sour.

Coffee
In the eighteenth century coffee was more popular in London than any other global location. Coffee was also thought to increase the reproductive capabilities of men.

Peas
Peas were an integral part of the English diet during the eighteenth century because people could dry them, and thus keep them in storage for a considerable time.

Gruel
This common eighteenth-century British dish was composed of boiled oatmeal with a little butter. Interestingly, it also often contained alcoholic beverages, especially wine. This dish was popular because it helped compensate for the lack of central heating in draughty houses.

4 GEORGE POLAIN (1809-1849)

4.1 Historical Context

A window on the past

To this point, the story of our direct ancestors has been primarily lists of names and dates. For this generation it all changes and that is because the story centres around a particular place at a particular time.

The place is a small, congested and run down part of Bethnal Green, near Shoreditch. It was a notorious slum and inhabited by the desperately poor and the criminal. It was referred to as **"*The Old Nichol*"**, named after the original developer of the estate.

To help the reader orientate themselves with the area (many of the road names are the same and some buildings, especially the churches, still remain) **Appendix H** Maps B1 to B10 show the area as it evolved over the years.

In 1801, the population of Greater London was 1 million. By 1851 it was 2.3 million which spurred a high demand for cheap housing.

The London slums became notorious for overcrowding, unsanitary and squalid living conditions. Most well-off Victorians believed that the slums were the outcome of laziness, sin and vice of the lower classes. However, a number of socially conscious writers and reformers argued that the growth of slums was caused by poverty, unemployment, social exclusion and homelessness.

Whitechapel was the hub of the Victorian East End. By the end of the seventeenth century it was a relatively prosperous district. However, some of its areas began to deteriorate in the mid eighteenth century, and in the second half of the nineteenth century they became overcrowded and crime infested.

'The Nichol' was one of a number of estates in the area built by private developers. Originally built as low cost housing for the poor of the East End, the condition of the buildings had deteriorated over the years and by the 1840s the area was notorious as one of the worst slums in London.

'The Nichol' was situated between High Street, Shoreditch, and Bethnal Green, and to the south was isolated from the rest of the city by the Great Eastern rail lines to Broad Street and the GER Goods Station in (what had been) Church Street by 1890. It consisted of 20 narrow streets containing 730 dilapidated terraced houses which were inhabited by up to 30,000 people. In was in the heart of the Old Nichol that George Polain, his wife Elizabeth and their 6 children lived.

The London County Council (LCC) decided to clear the Nichol slums in the 1890s, and the first council housing development in Britain, called the Boundary Estate, was built in its place shortly before 1900.

A more detailed description of the Nichol estate is included in **Appendix A,** together with contemporary descriptions of the living conditions.

The Boundary Road Estate today

Timelines

1820s

- George III dies and is succeeded by George IV
- World's first steam locomotive passenger service begins
- Robert Peel sets up the Metropolitan Police
- Food prices high due to "corn laws" designed to benefit landlord growers.
- The right to strike is granted and worker's unions are allowed.

1830s

- George IV dies and is succeeded by his brother William IV
- Parliament passes a bill to abolish slavery in the British empire
- Victoria comes to the throne after the death of William IV
- Charles Dicken's Oliver Twist is published
- Work for children over 9 is limited to 9-12 hours a day, and some schooling for children under 13.
- Daguerre invents rudimentary photography.
- Compulsory registration of Births, Deaths and Marriages
- Steamship service begins on the Atlantic with an average crossing time of 15 days.

1840s

- Income tax is introduced for the first time during peacetime
- The Corn Laws are repealed. Irish famine.
- France removes its monarch and becomes a republic.
- Brunel's *"Great Britain"* is launched
- Canada is awarded independence from Britain.
- Cholera is linked to water supplies.

A Brief & Incomplete Family History

1850s

- Britain and France declare war on Russia and the Crimean War begins
- The Great Exhibition of Works of Industry of all Nations showcasing Jacquard looms (patterns recorded on punch cards), American reaping machines, and an electric telegraph.
- Indian Mutiny and the Opium War in China
- The Panama Railway opens
- The Origin of Species by Darwin is published and met with harsh criticism.

Famous People

1820-1910	Florence Nightingale
1828-1910	Leo Tolstoy
1834-1896	William Morris
1837-1876	Wild Bill Hickok
1846-1917	Buffalo Bill Cody
1847-1931	Thomas Edison
1848-1929	Wyatt Earp

Victoria (1837-1901)

4.2 George's Family

George and Elizabeth

According to his baptism records, **George** Peter was born on 26th April 1809 and baptised in St. Matthews on 9th July 1809.

George married **Elizabeth** Dabbs on 11th December 1831 at St. Johns, Hackney. Elizabeth was born in Thomas Street, now known as Bacon Street, just off Brick Lane and to the south of Bethnal Green Road. George and Elizabeth were both 22 years old.

At the time of the birth of their first child in 1834, they were living at 17, (Old) Castle Street, Bethnal Green.

There were a number of streets called Castle or Old / New Castle Street (or possibly Newcastle Street!) about 1830 and 1840 in East London, but I presume this address actually refers to the Castle Street that was just behind St. Leonard's Church on Shoreditch High Street. According to a contemporary map their house backed onto a timber yard and later the street became known as Virginia Road.

This was in the northern part of the area known as the *'Old Nichol'*. There is more information on this district in **Appendix A** as this is our window onto their world.

Over the years there were a number of 'improvement' schemes in the *'Old Nichol'* that actually made the lives of the inhabitants worse. Improvements over the years included a new church, new schools and some road widening schemes, but each improvement displaced people and reduced the number of houses available for poor people to rent.

Sometime between 1837 and 1849, George and his family moved to 21, Half Nichol Street. In various publications of the time this was also referred to as Half Nicol or Half Nicoll's Street but the use of the spelling 'Nichol' goes back to the original land developer's name in the 1700s. This was no more than a hundred yards from the house they had previously rented in on Castle Street.

George died on 13th August 1849 at the age of 40. His death certificate states that he died of English Cholera (5 days) and Asiatic Cholera (11 hours). He was buried at St. Matthews, Bethnal Green. **Appendix A** contains information about conditions in Half Nichol Street (and specifically at #21) which will help explain the cause of George's death.

The record of his burial show George was employed as a silk weaver, although whether he was actively employed as such is debatable, considering the decline of the silk industry due to the availability of printed cotton.

At the time of the 1851 census Elizabeth was still living in Half Nichol Street. Based on modern maps, contemporary maps and the number of houses in the street, we can calculate that a typical house in Half Nichol Street was 15 foot wide. Allowing for the stairs, corridors and fire places, individual rooms at the front of the downstairs would be about 10 foot wide.

The 1851 census shows that the house in Half Nichol Street had 4 families living in 4 rooms. George's widow, Elizabeth, lived in one room with 3 of her sons and 1 daughter. Of the other residents of 21 Half Nichol Street, one family had 4 people living in one room, another had 5 in one room. The last room served as a home and workshop for a carpenter, his wife and their 5 children. 21 people lived in the one small house.

Looking at the census returns for other houses in Half Nichol Street, this many people in one house appears fairly normal.

When the children had all moved away and she was on her own, Elizabeth was taken in by the **French Hospital** (for the Descendents of French Protestants) in Victoria Park. She died in May 1879 at the age of 70 and was buried in Ilford on 7th June.

The French Hospital ended up as home to a number of our ancestors. **Appendix D** contains some of the history of this charity (which still exists).

A Brief & Incomplete Family History

George's Children

We believe George and Elizabeth had 6 children, 4 of them boys, between 1834 and 1849.

- **George Thomas** was born in (Old) Castle Street on the 18th September 1834.

    In the 1851 census his job was listed as Errand Boy. He married Emma King at St. Thomas's Church, Bethnal Green on 4th September 1854. George was 20 years old and Emma was 2 years younger. Their first child was born in 1856 and over the next 25 years they had another 10 children. They had 5 boys.

    - **George Thomas** (junior) was born in 1856 but died within a year.
    - **Charles James** was born in 1857 in Half Nichol Street and emigrated to Melbourne, Australia where he married Mary Annie Clark from Tasmania. They lived initially in Footscray, Victoria and had 7 children but Charles died in 1899 in Perth at the age of 32. Mary lived on to the age of 80 and died in Rivervale, Perth in 1943.
    - **Harriet Elizabeth** was born in 1865 in Trafalgar Street and she married John Flude in 1892 in Old Street, London. They had four girls and one boy. Harriet died on 11th November 1918 (the same day that the Great War finished) in Islington, but John lived till 1965, to the surprising old age of 97.
    - **Claude** was born about 1868. He married Charlotte and had 4 children. For reasons that are unclear he seems to have adopted the POLAINE spelling.
    - **Pauline** was born about 1873 and married James Bingham in December 1898. Pauline died in 1944.
    - **Emma Elizabeth** was born about 1875 and married William Philp. There is no further information on Emma.

    George and Emma had 5 other children's births registered between 1870 and 1881. They were **Mary**, **Polly**, **Claude**, **Adelaide** and **George**. We have no further information on these individuals and it is possible some or all of them died in infancy.

    By 1871, George had moved to 9, Trafalgar Street.

    Trafalgar Street was the name in the early part of the 18th Century for the road at the eastern end of Half Nichol Street, beyond the junction with Nichol Row. It seems the name had fallen out of favour by the 1880s-although it still appeared on some maps. On the corner of Trafalgar Street and Sarah Street was "The Lord Nelson" pub so we can presume there was a ready supply of ale available.

    Before the time of the next census in 1881, the family had moved to 100, Warner Place. By 1891, George and Emma had moved to New Tyrson Street and within 10 years had moved again to Barnel Road, both in Bethnal Green. We cannot identify either of the two locations. George and Emma eventually moved into the Almshouses in Parminter Street some time before 1911. These buildings were destroyed by a V2 rocket during February 1945, but George and Emma were long gone by that time.

Over the 60 years of census records available, George seems to have had a variety of jobs, ranging from Errand Boy as a youth, to Ivory Cutter, Comb Maker and Gas Stoker. It is possible the jobs of Ivory Cutter and Comb Maker are actually the same thing. At the time there was a vogue for carved ladies hair combs made from ivory. The last job relates to the days when gas was produced from heating coal in stoking ovens.

George and Emma had a long life together. Emma died in 1922 and George died in 1924 at the age of 89. George was buried in Abney Park Cemetery, London

- **Elizabeth Rebecca** was born in December 1836 while the family lived in (Old) Castle Street. She married Charles Carlier (a name that has cropped up before from the Polain family's Huguenot history) in 1856 in Haggerston, East London. Together they had 8 children and Elizabeth died on 13th December 1920 at the French Hospital (for descendents of French Protestants), near Victoria Park.

- **William John** was born in 1840. In the 1851 census William was shown as a Scholar. Whether he was actually at school is of course a different matter as the ragged schools in the Nichol required payment and children's ages were frequently inflated to avoid the laws restricting the employment of children. He married Jane Ann (?) in 1862.

  o They had 4 children but nothing is known about **Harriet**, **George** and **Jane** except their birth dates.

  o The exception is **William James** who was born about 1866 and married Priscilla Georgina Thomas in 1886. They had 6 children.

  William died in Southwark in 1903, at the age of 63.

- **Charles** was born about 1842 but we have no further information on him. There is no mention of Charles in the census, who at this time would also have been about 10, so we can only presume he died some time before 1851.

- **John William** was born about 1842 and emigrated to Australia. He married Maria Fanny Hawksley in 1866 in Adelaide and they had 7 children. John died in 1918 and Maria died 10 years later.

- **Joseph William George** was born in 1849 and married Maria Ann Boxell at the age of 21. The story of his family is contained in the next section as he was a direct ancestor of this family.

A Brief & Incomplete Family History

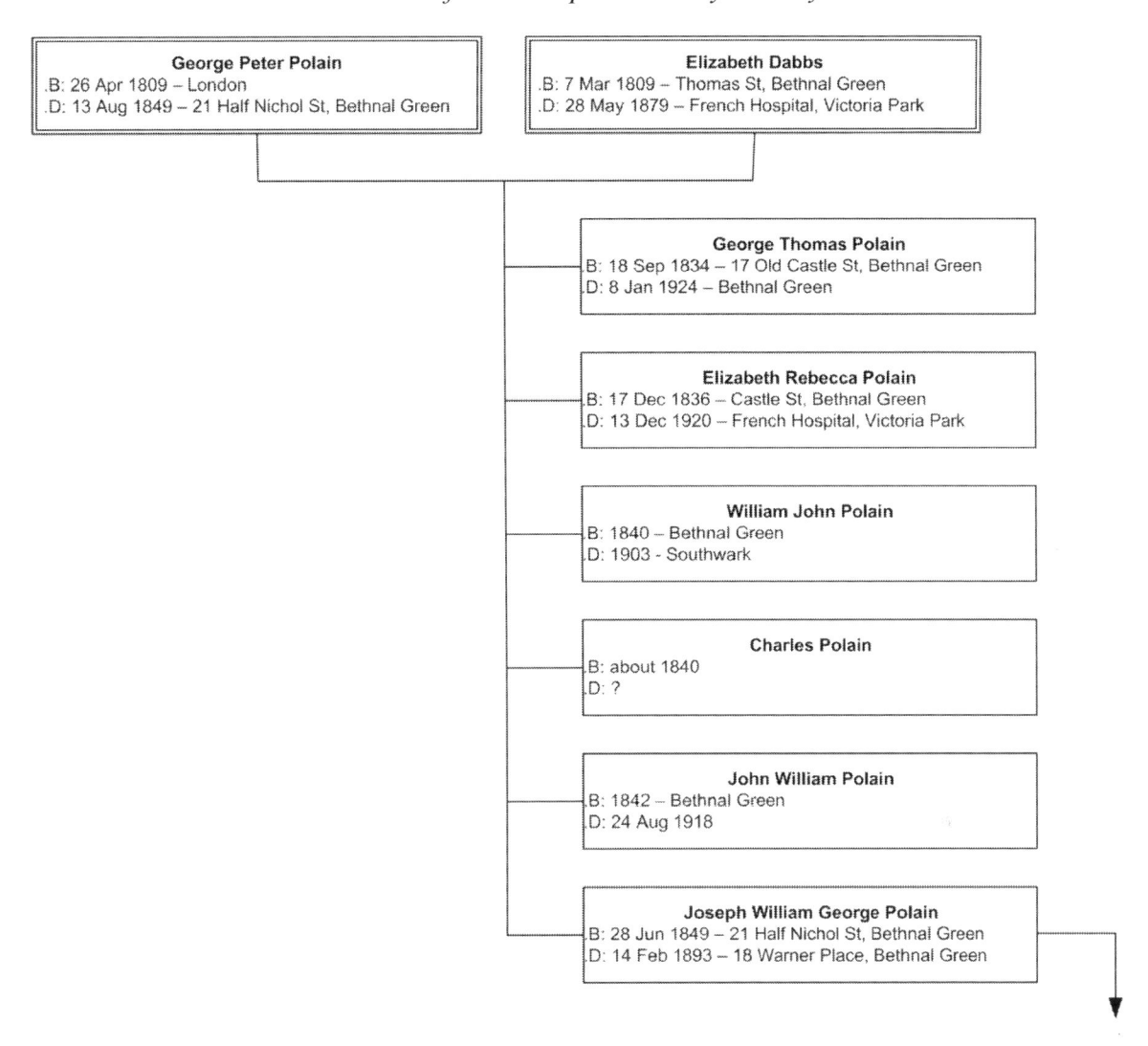

George Peter Polain
B: 26 Apr 1809 – London
D: 13 Aug 1849 – 21 Half Nichol St, Bethnal Green

Elizabeth Dabbs
B: 7 Mar 1809 – Thomas St, Bethnal Green
D: 28 May 1879 – French Hospital, Victoria Park

George Thomas Polain
B: 18 Sep 1834 – 17 Old Castle St, Bethnal Green
D: 8 Jan 1924 – Bethnal Green

Elizabeth Rebecca Polain
B: 17 Dec 1836 – Castle St, Bethnal Green
D: 13 Dec 1920 – French Hospital, Victoria Park

William John Polain
B: 1840 – Bethnal Green
D: 1903 - Southwark

Charles Polain
B: about 1840
D: ?

John William Polain
B: 1842 – Bethnal Green
D: 24 Aug 1918

Joseph William George Polain
B: 28 Jun 1849 – 21 Half Nichol St, Bethnal Green
D: 14 Feb 1893 – 18 Warner Place, Bethnal Green

George's family

4.3 Bits of the Jigsaw

Education

Since the early 1800s, Sunday schools had provided the only education for children from poor families. These were latter followed by Ragged schools, which were charitable organisations dedicated to the free education of destitute children. Such children, it was argued, were often excluded from Sunday School education because of their unkempt appearance and often challenging behaviour.

There were penny schools and 'ragged schools' on the Nichol estate so children could get some education, assuming the breadwinner could afford to pay for the school. As soon as possible the children would be working (or stealing) to support the family.

At the corner of Old Nichol Street and Nichol's Row there was a 'Ragged School', next door to the Mission Hall. The school consisted of a number of small, single storey buildings and a 2/3 storey building

The London Ragged Schools Union was established in April 1844 to combine resources in the city, providing free education, food, clothing, lodging and other home missionary services for poor children. The children only had very ragged clothes to wear and they rarely had shoes. In other words, they did not own clothing suitable to attend any other kind of school

Working in the poorest districts, teachers (who were often local working people) initially utilized stables, lofts, and railway arches for their classes. The majority of teachers were voluntary, although a small number were employed. There was an emphasis on reading, writing, arithmetic, and study of the Bible. It is estimated that about 300,000 children went through the London ragged schools between 1844 and 1881.

The London Ragged Schools Union charity was supported by Charles Dickens and Dr Barnardo, but the number of Ragged Schools declined after Board Schools were introduced after 1870.

Board Schools were elementary schools, free from religious teaching. The schools were generally financed by a local authority but lessons were not free except for the poorest pupils. Board Schools were abolished in 1902 and replaced with local education authorities.

At the junction of Sarah Street and Mead Street and only 40 yards from the Ragged School a Board School was established before the demolition of the housing started.

Slumming

To add insult to injury to the poor people who lived in the Nichol, it became a popular destination for 'slumming'. For some, slumming was a peculiar form of tourism motivated by curiosity, excitement and thrill. Others were motivated by moral, religious and altruistic reasons such as religious missionaries, charity workers, social investigators and writers.

Jack London, an American writer, travelled to England just to stay 'undercover' in the East End for 6 weeks to provide the material for a book, despite there being plenty of similar slums in New York.

Campaigning

The conditions in the Nichol raised some very uncomfortable questions for the wealthy and middle classes of Britain and there were no easy or quick solutions.

- Did the poor create the conditions in which they lived or did their poverty come from the living conditions they were forced to endure?
- Who were the "deserving poor" and who were the "undeserving poor"?
- Did drunkenness cause the low incomes and ill health of the area's residents or was drunkenness a direct consequence of the living conditions?

Posed photographs of children, known as "Shoreditch Nippers" were used by charities and reforming activists to gain support. Although these photos are not labelled as such it is probably the reason they were taken.

The newspapers campaigned for a solution to the problems so there is a large quantity of information available about the Nichol between 1840 and 1890. In addition, the plight of the poor and the street urchins became popularised in books and novels by Charles Dickens and others.

A thinly disguised description of the Nichol even featured in a popular book called "**Child of the Jago**" by Arthur Morrison. This is still available on line.

As the Nichol was so well documented at the time, there are vivid contemporary accounts of the people and the conditions they lived in. Many of these publications are available on the internet, and fascinating (and horrifying) reading they make. See the chemical analysis of ice cream made in one of the backstreet workshops-you will never look at an ice cream cone the same way again!

I have included some of the more pertinent (and less offensive) descriptions in **Appendix A.**

Slum Clearance

The first major slum clearance act of the new London Corporation was to compulsorily purchase the houses in the Nichol and to demolish the buildings. A new estate of model housing was built in its place and still exists (see the buildings around Arnold Circus where the bandstand is). It was named the Boundary Estate after Boundary Street-which was the boundary between the parishes of St. Leonards and St. Matthews.

At the time it was claimed that 6,000 people had to be forcibly removed when the houses in the old streets were demolished.

However, the price of the new rooms in the Boundary Estate was higher than the old residents could have afforded so all that happened was that the desperately poor people from the Nichol were displaced to other deprived areas of London.

The designers of the new estate retained only Boundary Street in the west and Mount Street in the east, though they widened both to 40 ft (12 m). Old Nichol Street was also widened and extended to Mount Street, then renamed Swanfield Street. They also included 50 feet wide tree lined streets to radiate from an ornamental space called Arnold Circus-complete with bandstand.

The flats remain and are Grade II listed, together with the bandstand. In their day, they were revolutionary in their provision of facilities for residents. Today, despite the lack of some modern amenities they remain popular with tenants and there is an active community.

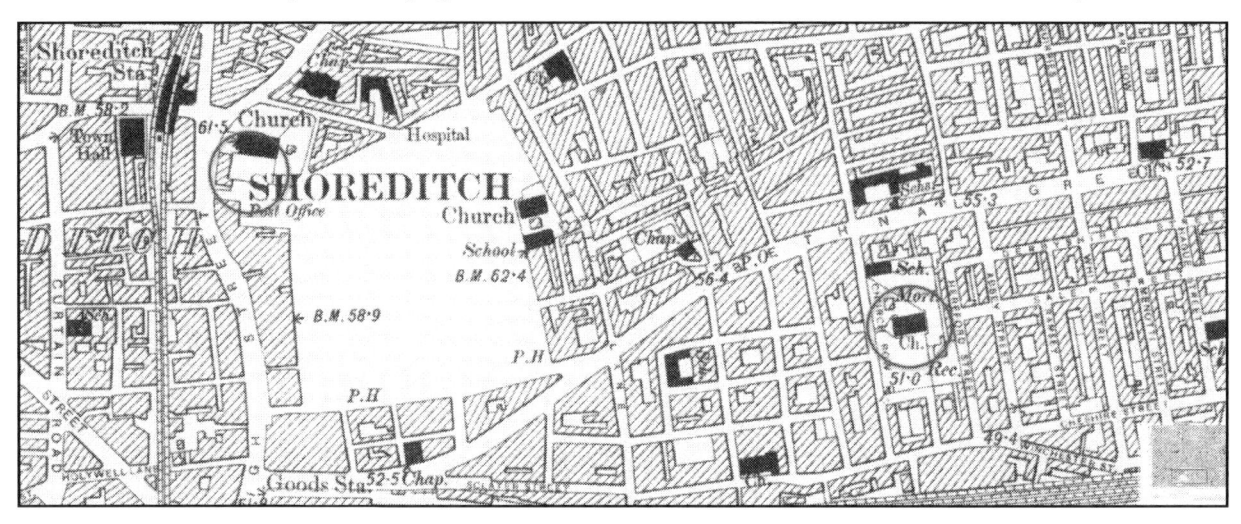

MAP 6 - The 'Nichol' district (about 1900), showing the extent of the demolition

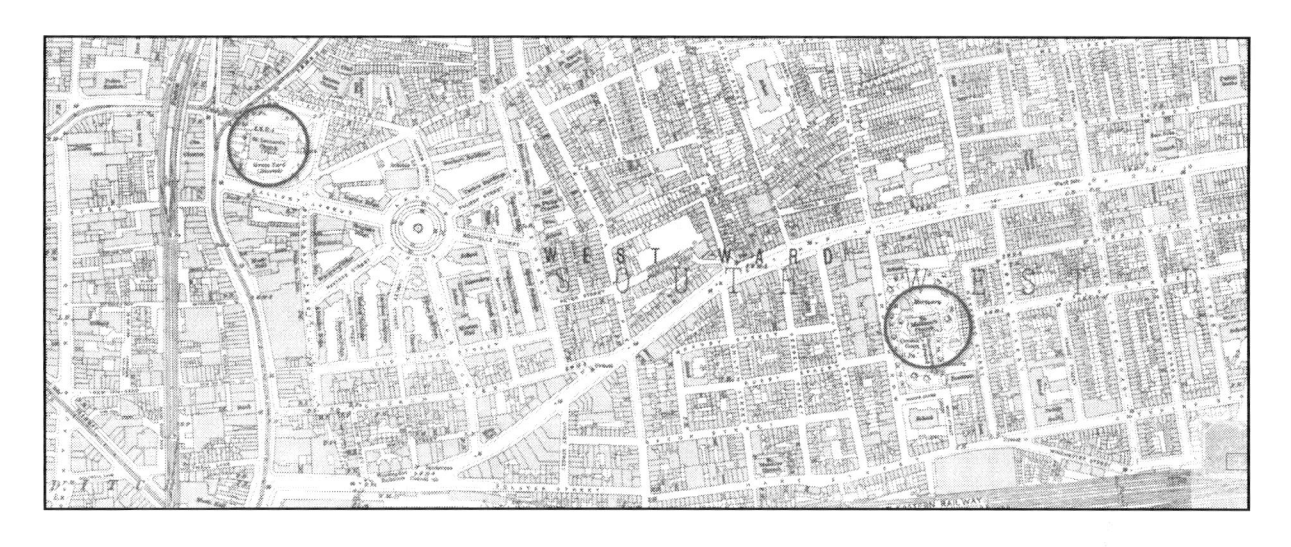

MAP 7 - The Boundary Road estate after redevelopment of the area (about 1910.

Appendix H contains larger scale versions of these maps

5 JOSEPH POLAIN   (1849-1893)

5.1 Historical Context

A Growing City

Between 1850 and the end of the 19th century, London was transformed into the world's largest city and capital of the British Empire. During this period, London became a global political, financial, and trading capital.

London skyline in 1880

London was both the world's largest port and a major shipbuilding centre for the entire 19th century. In the East End there were the West India Docks, the East India Docks as well as London Docks in Wapping. With the eclipse of the sailing ship by the steamship in mid-century, tonnages grew larger and the shallow docks nearer the city were too small for mooring them. In response, the Royal Victoria Dock, the Millwall Dock, the Royal Albert Dock and the Port of Tilbury were built.

Shipping in the Port of London supported a vast army of transport and warehouse workers, who characteristically attended the "call-on" each morning at the entrances to the docks to be assigned work for the day. This type of work was low-paid and highly unstable, drying up depending on the season and the vagaries of world trade. The poverty of the dock workers and growing trade union activism coalesced into the Great Strike of 1889.

The Regents Canal was the only canal link to the Thames, connecting a vital shipping outlet with the great industrial cities of The Midlands. The Regents Canal became a huge success, but on a local rather than a national level because it facilitated the localized transport of goods like coal, timber, and other building materials around London. Easy access to coal shipments from northeast England via the Port of London meant that a profusion of industries along the Regent's Canal, especially gasworks, and later electricity generating plants

The City of London's importance as a financial centre increased substantially over the course of the 19th century. The City's strengths in banking, stock brokerage, and shipping insurance made it the natural channel for a huge rise in capital investment.

The result of the shift to financial services in the City was that, even while its residential population was ebbing in favour of the suburbs it retained its traditional role as the centre of English commerce.

London's great expansion in the 19th Century was driven by housing growth to accommodate the rapidly expanding population of the city. The growth of transport in London in this period fuelled the outward expansion of suburbs. Suburbs varied enormously in character and in the relative wealth of their inhabitants, with terraced, semi-detached and detached housing all developed in a multitude of styles, with an almost endless variation in the layout of streets, gardens and homes.

Mass demolition of slums just displaced existing residents because the new dwellings built by private developers were often far too expensive for the previous inhabitants to afford. In the mid to late 19th century, charities like the Peabody Trust focused on building adequate housing for the working classes at affordable rates. The Metropolitan Board of Works was empowered to undertake clearances and to enforce legislation.

The East End of London, with an economy oriented around the Docklands and the industries clustered along the Thames and the River Lea, had long been an area of working poor. Life for the poor was immortalized by Charles Dickens in such novels as Oliver Twist.

Mass transport was becoming ever more important

within the city as its population increased. The first horse-drawn omnibuses entered service in London in 1829 but by 1854 there were 3,000 of them in service, each carrying an average of 300 passengers per day.

The two-wheeled hansom cab, first seen in 1834, was the most common type of cab on London's roads throughout the Victorian era, in addition to the coaches, private carriages, coal-wagons, and tradesman's vehicles which crowded the roads.

From the 1870s onwards, Londoners also had access to a developing tram network. By 1893 there were about 1,000 tram cars across 135 miles of track.

19th century London was transformed by the coming of the railways. A new network of metropolitan railways allowed the development of suburbs from which middle-class and wealthy people could commute. While this spurred the massive outward growth of the city, London's growth also exacerbated the class divide, as the wealthier classes escaped to the suburbs, leaving the poor to inhabit the inner city areas.

By 1865 there were 12 principal railway termini. The Cheap Trains Act 1883 helped poorer Londoners to relocate, by guaranteeing cheap fares and removing a duty imposed on fares since 1844. The new working class suburbs created as a result included West Ham, Walthamstow, Kilburn, and Willesden.

With traffic congestion on London's roads becoming more and more serious, proposals for underground railways to ease the pressure on street traffic were first mooted in the 1840s. The completion of the Metropolitan Railway in 1863 inaugurated the world's oldest mass transit system, the London Underground.

There was a flurry of bridge-building along the Thames. In 1800 there were only three bridges connecting Westminster and the City to the south bank: Westminster Bridge, Blackfriars Bridge, and the ancient London Bridge. Old London Bridge, whose 20 piers dated back to the 13th century, so impeded the flow of the river that it could not accommodate modern traffic levels. It was the first to be replaced, by a 49-foot wide granite bridge with five supporting arches. "New" London Bridge was built from 1824 to 1831, with the adjacent "Old" London Bridge fully dismantled by 1832.

The impetus for this building was London's massive population growth, which put a constant strain on existing communications between the north and south banks. This resulted in the commission of Tower Bridge in 1885. It was an engineering marvel which solved the conundrum of how to bridge the Thames downriver from London Bridge without inhibiting shipping.

Timelines

1860s

- William Gladstone becomes prime minister for the first time
- The American Civil War.
- A Second Reform Bill doubled the electorate.
- Bessemer improves steel production.
- First subways are built under London.
- Clipper ships further improve sea travel.
- Undersea transatlantic telegraph joins US and Britain.

1870s

- Trade unions become legal. Work week limited to 56.5 hours.
- Inventions of telephone, phonograph, and incandescent light bulb.
- Victoria is declared empress of India
- The Second Afghan War, British troops entered Afghanistan
- Battle of Isandhlwana and Rorke's Drift in southern Africa

1880s

- GMT adopted throughout the UK; Gunfight at the OK Coral
- Parcel post starts in Britain
- Education becomes compulsory for children under ten
- Married women obtain the right to acquire their own property
- First car built by Benz; Daimler builds first motorcycle
- Buffalo Bills Cody's Wild West Show opens in London
- First Kodak roll film camera sold by George Eastman brings photography to the masses.

Famous People

1854-1900	Oscar Wilde
1856-1943	Nikola Tesla
1858-1928	Emmeline Pankhurst
1863-1947	Henry Ford
1865-1936	Rudyard Kipling
1867-1934	Marie Curie
1870-1924	Lenin
1874-1965	Winston Churchill
1878-1953	Stalin

Edward VII (1901-1910)

5.2 Joseph's Family

Joseph and Maria

Joseph William was born on 28 June 1849, whilst his parents lived at 21, Half Nichol Street, Bethnal Green. He married **Maria Ann** Boxell on the 9th October 1870 at St. Jude's Church. The Marriage Certificate gives Maria's full name as "Maria Horn St. Georgina Ann"-where this name comes from is unclear but the family (at least her granddaughter) always knew her as Maria.

Maria was born in Austin Street, a few hundred yards away from where Joseph lived. It seems that in those times, you didn't cast your net very wide when looking for partners for life.

Joseph's Children

Joseph and Maria's first child was born in 1872 and they had another 8 children in the following 20 years.

- **Joseph William George** was born in 1872 but few records of him or his family remain. He married Sarah about 1893. They had one child, Elizabeth Violet, in 1895. Joseph (junior) died in Epping in 1959.
- **Maria Ann** was born in 1874 and married Thomas Charles Gray about December 1895. There is a record of a single child, Harold, born about 1899, but no other records of the family remain.
- **Ester** was born in 1878. She married Walter Clarke and died November 1926. There is no record of any children

- **Maude Emily** was born 1882. She married Mr. Master and they had at least 2 children. She died in 1957 and was buried at Manor Park Cemetery.
- **Arthur Henry** was born in 18878 and died in Poplar in 1929. There is no record of any surviving children.
- **Ethel Lillian** (Lillie) was born in 1891. She married George Dominic Brugnoli in 1916 and they lived for some years at 102, Old Bethnal Green Road. They had 5 children. George died in 1945 but Lillian survived him by 20 years. She died whilst living at 1, Nicholas Road, Stepney on 8th October 1965, at the age of 74.
- **Cecil Percival** was born in 1892. He had a daughter, Phyllis, and he died in 1971 in Hackney.

From the list of Joseph and Maria's children above, there are two exclusions and they are dealt with separately in the next section because they directly impact on the rest of this family's story.

- Joseph's son **John Albert** was the father of William (Bill) Polain, who married Violet Stevenson in 1939.
- Joseph's daughter **Florence Eliza** was the mother of Violet Stevenson, who married Bill Polain in 1939.

Therefore Violet was John Albert's niece. Bill was Florence Eliza's nephew and Vi and Bill were cousins. Phew!

5.3 Bits of the Jigsaw

Puzzles and explanations

One of the problems with family histories is that many official records are only available after being sealed for 100 years. For instance, the 1921 census was not released until 2021. There is therefore sometimes a gap between the verbal family history as passed on by Gran and Granddad and the official records.

The current generation of this branch of the POLAINs in the UK is very thin on the ground and we seem to have lost track over the years of other branches of the family, even if they appear to be living fairly locally. In these cases the only way to try to fill the gaps in the family is to approach every POLAIN in the UK telephone book and ask about their parentage.

This may not be generally acceptable when approached by a complete stranger and we have to accept that any plotting of the family tree is going to have limitations and gaps.

A few years ago when I had some spare time I went through all the Births, Marriage and Death Index books up to the year 1910. What I found was a large number of POLAINs that I couldn't identify or even work out where they could fit in.

A Brief & Incomplete Family History

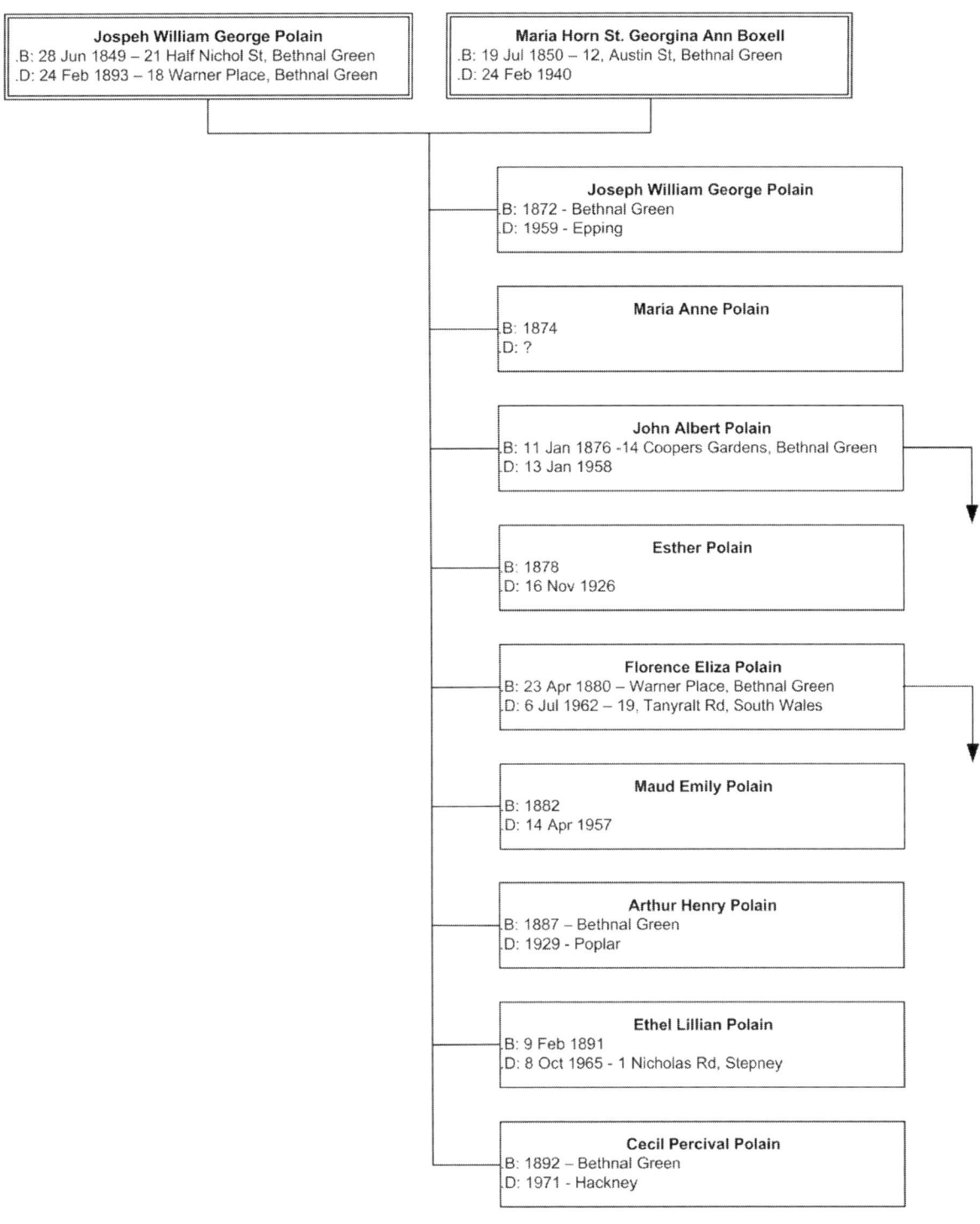

Joseph William George Polain
B: 28 Jun 1849 – 21 Half Nichol St, Bethnal Green
D: 24 Feb 1893 – 18 Warner Place, Bethnal Green

Maria Horn St. Georgina Ann Boxell
B: 19 Jul 1850 – 12, Austin St, Bethnal Green
D: 24 Feb 1940

- **Joseph William George Polain**
  B: 1872 - Bethnal Green
  D: 1959 - Epping

- **Maria Anne Polain**
  B: 1874
  D: ?

- **John Albert Polain**
  B: 11 Jan 1876 - 14 Coopers Gardens, Bethnal Green
  D: 13 Jan 1958

- **Esther Polain**
  B: 1878
  D: 16 Nov 1926

- **Florence Eliza Polain**
  B: 23 Apr 1880 – Warner Place, Bethnal Green
  D: 6 Jul 1962 – 19, Tanyralt Rd, South Wales

- **Maud Emily Polain**
  B: 1882
  D: 14 Apr 1957

- **Arthur Henry Polain**
  B: 1887 – Bethnal Green
  D: 1929 - Poplar

- **Ethel Lillian Polain**
  B: 9 Feb 1891
  D: 8 Oct 1965 - 1 Nicholas Rd, Stepney

- **Cecil Percival Polain**
  B: 1892 – Bethnal Green
  D: 1971 - Hackney

Joseph's family

A Brief & Incomplete Family History

For information, I include a list of the 'missing' POLAINs in **Appendix G,** and it is clear that we may be missing a whole branch of the Polain family, not just one or two individuals. It only takes a single male Polain not registered at birth, and after a couple of generations there could, quite literally, be dozens of POLAINs we cannot fit into the family tree.

This could be explained by some of the POLAINE branch of the family reverting to the original POLAIN spelling, but to sort that out would take a huge amount of detective work.

6 GRANDPARENTS

6.1 Historical Context

End of an Era

After the First Boer War in 1880-1881, the Boers refused to recognize the rights of the British citizens living in the Transvaal, leading to the Second Boer War. Although the Boers had initial military successes, the war ended in May 1902 with a Boer surrender. It was a costly and unpopular war.

Victoria died at Osborne House on the Isle of Wight at the age of 81. As queen-empress she had ruled over almost a quarter of the world's population. Her death, coming so soon after the end of the 19th century, was the end of an era.

Ships grew larger and faster. Sail was entirely displaced by steam. International travel, and large scale immigration to the colonies and America, became feasible. In 1912, RMS Titanic sank with the loss of 1,496 lives-a radio distress message was sent using the newly designed Marconi transmitters but not received in time by other ships in the area.

London became the center for the suffrage movement spearheaded by Emmeline Pankhurst. Protests and demonstrations intensified, reaching a peak between 1912 and 1914 as the movement became more militant. In 1913, Emily Davison ran out in front of the King's horse at the Epsom Derby and was killed.

The years between Queen Victoria's death in 1901 and the start of the First World War were years of growth and general prosperity, though the extreme inequalities which had characterized Victorian London continued. By 1911 over 7 million Britons lived in London.

The First World War started on 28th July 1914. It was to last over 4 years and cost between 15 to 22 million lives. Prior to the war, Britain was the world's economic superpower. The world would never be the same again.

Due to the shortage of male labour, women's employment went from 23% of the working age population in 1914 to 47% in 1918. The largest employer of women was the munitions industries.

Despite the huge role women played in the maintenance of the economy, they still only received around two-thirds of the pay that men received for the same jobs.

During World War I, London experienced 11 airship raids. By 1917, British success at shooting down airships persuaded the German military to instead use aeroplanes. In June 1917 the largest World War I air raid on London was carried out, resulting in about 160 deaths. Further raids followed during 1917 and 1918. However, by May 1918 British air defences had improved sufficiently to start inflicting heavy German losses, and this persuaded Germany to call the raids off.

There was much rebuilding in Central London during the Edwardian years. Much of the construction was delayed by the Great War and completed in the 1920s.

Regent Street, originally constructed in the 1820s was rebuilt entirely between 1905 and 1927. The Mall was re-envisioned as a grand parade route for state pageantry, which involved the building of Admiralty Arch and the erection of the Victoria Memorial. In Holborn, the slum area known as Clare Market was demolished to make way for Kingsway with an underground tramway tunnel. Aldwych, the crescent-shaped road connecting Kingsway with the Strand, was lined with new theatres and hotels.

The early 20th century saw London's urban areas grow faster than at any point before. Most of the development was expansion into Essex, Hertfordshire, Kent, Middlesex and Surrey. The rapid expansion of London during this period swallowed up large swathes of countryside.

There was a rapid expansion and modernisation of the transport networks. A large tram network was constructed by the London County Council and the first motorbus service began in the 1900s. New railway lines were constructed and commuting from the suburbs became a reality for working people.

At the beginning of this period, horse drawn carriages, carts and buses were the standard form of transport. By the 1920s, they were displaced by motor transport, but private car ownership was still a rarity.

The first flight, by the Wright Brothers at Kitty Hawk was in 1903. A.V. Roe made the first British powered flight in a triplane in 1908 at Walthamstow Marshes. Louis Bleriot, was the first to fly across the English Channel, 21 miles from Calais to Dover. Especially during the war years, development of aircraft was rapid and by 1920 London's first international airport, Croydon, was operational.

Timelines

1890s

- Edison patents motion picture cameras
- Labour Party founded; Henry Ford's first car
- Tower Bridge over the Thames opens.
- Marconi invents wireless telegraphy
- Zip fasteners invented.
- Zeppelin airship
- First circumnavigation by Joshua Slocum.
- Second Boer War begins in South Africa

1900s

- Boxer rising in Peking; School leaving age raised to 14; Central Line opens
- Queen Victoria dies; first radio transmission across the Atlantic
- First flight by the Wright brothers. First airship flies over London
- First colour photographs. Ford makes the Model T
- Ernest Shackleton finds magnetic South Pole. Bleriot flies across the English Channel

1910s

- *"Titanic"* sinks on maiden voyage
- Emily Davidson, a suffragette, runs in front of the King's horse and dies
- Archduke Franz Ferdinand is assassinated in Sarajevo
- Britain declares war on Germany in response to the invasion of Belgium
- Bolsheviks, under Vladimir Lenin, create a communist revolution in Russia
- World War One ends when Germany signs an armistice

1920s

- Lady Astor becomes the first woman to take her seat in parliament; Women at Oxford University are allowed to receive degrees; All women over the age of 21 get the vote
- Ramsay Macdonald becomes the first Labour prime minister
- John Logie Baird gives the first public demonstration of television
- Alexander Fleming discovers penicillin
- Wall Street Crash sparks the Great Depression

Famous People

Famous people born between 1880 and 1920.

1881-1973	Picasso
1889-1977	Charlie Chaplin
1889-1945	Hitler
1897-1939	Amelia Earhart
1898-1988	Enzo Ferrari
1899-1980	Alfred Hitchcock
1901-1966	Walt Disney
1903-1977	Bing Crosby
1907-1979	John Wayne
1911-2004	Ronald Reagan
1915-1998	Frank Sinatra
1916-2020	Kirk Douglas

Victoria (1837-1901)  *Edward VII (1901-1910)*  *George V (1910-1936)*

* * *

6.2 The POLAIN family

John Albert Polain (1876-1958)

Parents *Joseph William George **Polain** and Maria Ann **Polain** (nee Boxell)*
Siblings *Joseph (1872), Maria Ann, (1874), John Albert (1876), Esther (1878), Maud Emily (1882), Arthur Henry (1887), Ethal Lillian (1891) and Cecil Percival (1892)*

John Albert was born on 11th January in 1876 at 14 Coopers Gardens, Bethnal Green.

His father gave his occupation as Boot Maker on the birth certificate. By the time of the next census in 1881 when John was 5, the family had moved to 27 Warner Place, Bethnal Green.

By 1891 when John was 15, he was already working as a Rope Maker and living with his mother and father at 18, Warner Place.

Jane Holloway (1878-1939)

Parents *No record*
Siblings *No record*

Jane Holloway was born in 1878 in Bethnal Green. Jane was 2 years younger than John and lived with her parents and brother at 14, Collins Place (renamed Surat Street and long lost) in Bethnal Green. John and Jane married before 1896.

By 1901, John and Jane were living in Lincoln Street (now Brokesley Street) off Mile End Road (see **Appendix H** for more of the history of Brokesley Street).

The census shows that as well as their two eldest children, Maria's brother Joseph was living with them as a lodger.

John's house backed onto the City of London Union Infirmary (up until the 1860s it had been the Workhouse, but as other Workhouses were built, these buildings became London Union's hospital). John's occupation as a rope maker puzzled me until I found an old rope walk on the south side of Tower Hamlets Cemetery in what is now Ropery Street (the cemetery is literally at the end of the street and the shape of a rope factory is distinctive). So it is clear he moved to Lincoln Street to be closer to work. However, the factory disappeared from the maps within a few years so John would have needed to find a new occupation. (see **Appendix H** for views of John's home as it is today)

Before 1911, the family had moved to 33, Arkley Crescent in Walthamstow (off Markhouse Road - the area has since been redeveloped) and John was working as a labourer on the railways.

At that time, John and Jane had 5 children. The youngest, Alice, was just 3 but her older siblings, including her 13 year old big sister Jane, were all at school. Jane gave her occupation as a Boot Sewer, working from home. The house is described in the census return as having 3 rooms

Before 1938, they moved again to 42, Haroldstone Road in Walthamstow, where they rented a flat.

Jane died in August 1939 and was buried in Walthamstow Cemetery. John lived in Haroldstone Road until his death in 1958. He was buried in Walthamstow Cemetery.

Haroldstone Road as it is now

* * *

John & Jane's Children

- About 1897, **Jane** (junior) was born. She married Albert Nie and died in January 1953. They had no children.
- John was born about 1898 in Mile End. He married Elsie and they had 4 children:
    - **John** was born in 1923 and died in 1992
    - **Ron** was born in 1925 and died in 1991
    - **Elsie** and **Lily** - we have no dates or details for these ladies

  At the time of his death he was living in Gosport Road in Walthamstow.

- **Violet** May was born about 1904 and married Edward (Ted) Fallis. They lived in Ruislip, Middlesex (now the London borough of Hillingdon)and Ted worked for many years as a Policeman. They had two boys:
    - **John** (born 1930) became a car designer and worked for Ford in the UK, the USA and Europe, ending his career as Vice President. He married Pat but after they broke up he married Hella. John and Hella had a daughter, Claudia but John died of pancreatic cancer while he was living in Essex . Hella remarried and she and Claudia now live in Majorca.
    - **David** (born 1932) married Jean Emmett and after some years working at London Airport for BEA, he fulfilled his dream of moving to Northern Ireland to open a hotel. David and Jean had three children, Andrew, Victoria and Malcolm.
- **Thomas** was born in 1905. He married Mary Ward in 1930 in West Ham and 6 children were born in the following 13 years.
    - **Thomas** (junior) was born in 1932 and married Pamela Barham from Upminster . They had two children, Stephen and Kevin.
    - **Eileen** (born 1934) died in 1999.
    - **Kenneth** (born 1936), married Diane and had a boy, Darren
    - **Clifford** (born 1938), married Sylvia and they had a son, Gary
    - **Maureen** and **Vera** were born in 1944 and 1945 respectively. We have no further information.

  After they were married, Thomas and Mary lived in York Road, Walthamstow, but moved to Hornchurch before 1934. Mary died in 1975 and Thomas died 4 years later, in 1979.

- **Alice** was born in 1909 and died in 1926 at the age of 17.
- **William Alfred** (but known to everyone as Bill) was born in April 1912.

Bill was my father and we look at his life in a little more detail in the next chapter.

A Brief & Incomplete Family History

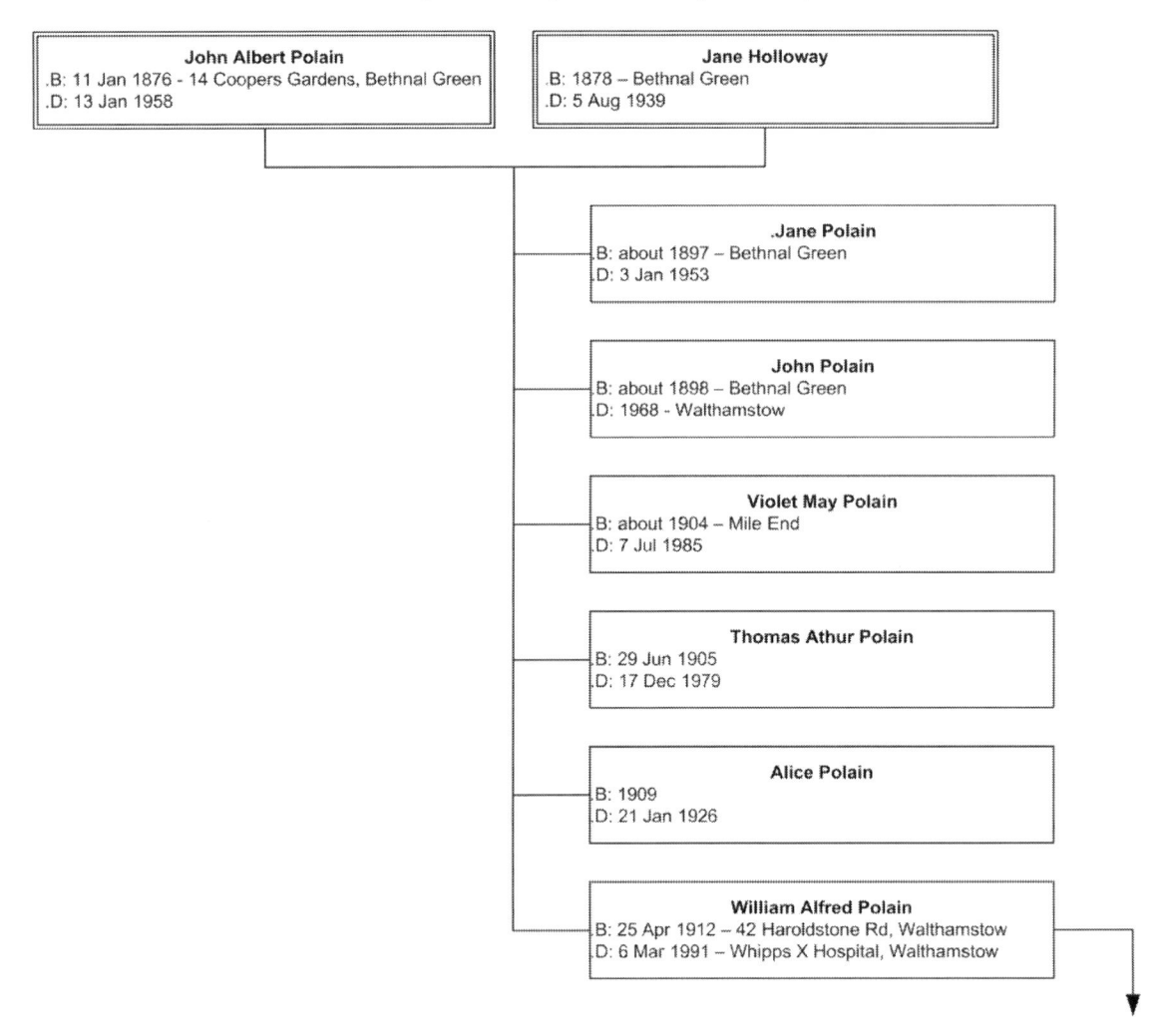

- **John Albert Polain**
  - B: 11 Jan 1876 - 14 Coopers Gardens, Bethnal Green
  - D: 13 Jan 1958

- **Jane Holloway**
  - B: 1878 – Bethnal Green
  - D: 5 Aug 1939

Children:

- **Jane Polain**
  - B: about 1897 – Bethnal Green
  - D: 3 Jan 1953

- **John Polain**
  - B: about 1898 – Bethnal Green
  - D: 1968 - Walthamstow

- **Violet May Polain**
  - B: about 1904 – Mile End
  - D: 7 Jul 1985

- **Thomas Athur Polain**
  - B: 29 Jun 1905
  - D: 17 Dec 1979

- **Alice Polain**
  - B: 1909
  - D: 21 Jan 1926

- **William Alfred Polain**
  - B: 25 Apr 1912 – 42 Haroldstone Rd, Walthamstow
  - D: 6 Mar 1991 – Whipps X Hospital, Walthamstow

John Albert's family

6.3 The STEVENSON family

William Henry Stevenson (1876-1940)

Parents   *Arthur William* **Stevenson** *and Emily* **Cannell**
Siblings   *Emily, Charles*

William Henry (**Harry**) was born on 28th May 1876 at 218, Old Ford Road, but by the time of the 1881 Census, he is shown as living at 200, Old Ford Road, Bethnal Green.

By 1891, his father, a Cabinet Maker, had remarried and the family had moved to 10, Lyte Street, Bethnal Green (this was just around the corner of the Waterloo Road Workhouse with 1,400 inmates-it wasn't until the mid 1930s the site was closed and the building demolished).

Harry's occupation at the age of 15 was recorded in the Census as "Tinker". At that time, there was only compulsory school attendance between the ages of 5 and 10, so children as young as 11 could legally work.

William joined the Royal Marine Light Infantry on the 1st June 1898 when he was 18 years old and 5' 6" tall. His service history states his previous job was as a labourer. He was given the service number 10342.

After basic training and an initial posting at Chatham, he embarked on **HMS Monarch** in November 1899 for South Africa, arriving 31st December, where the Boer War had just started. The Naval Brigade, formed from HM Ships Doris, Powerful and Monarch, was landed at Simonstown, South Africa. This brigade included the RMLI and RMA Detachments from these ships, a total of 190 Officers and men.

The Brigade was sent, with its four naval guns, to break through the Boer lines to effect the relief of Kimberley.

We have no details of William's service during the Boer war, but he was certainly involved in the actions at Driefonttein (March 1900) and Paardeberg (February 1900). For this he received the Queens South Africa Medal with 3 clasps.

By May, he was invalided back to hospital in Cape Town, presumably due to the sickness that was rife in the Colony. He returned to the UK on board the *SS Orotava*, a passenger steam ship. We can assume he was fully recovered by the time he got back to Chatham, as he was posted to **HMS Medusa**, a Marathon class cruiser moored at Chatham. However, this posting did not last long as he was transferred to **HMS Archer** in August 1900.

A Brief & Incomplete Family History

HMS Archer was built in 1885 as a torpedo cruiser. Torpedo cruisers were small, relatively fast ships intended to defend the fleet against attacks by hostile torpedo boats, while themselves being capable of attacking hostile fleets with torpedoes. She served on the Australia Station from 1900 until 1904.

The Concert Party of *HMS Archer*-probably taken while Harry was stationed in Sydney. His Service Record shows he was in Sydney when he took his 'musketry' refresher courses in 1902 and 1903. *HMS Archer* was a small vessel with a crew of about 100. She was an old ship and conditions for the crew were probably cramped and uncomfortable during the hot Australian summers.

After a number of brief postings to various the shore barracks of Chatham (he was in the Chatham division of the RMLI), William was assigned to **HMS Acheron** on 19th December 1904, just 6 days before his marriage to Flo Polain. William was on the *Acheron* for 2 years but he must have got leave at some point because his son Billy was born in 1906!

HMS Acheron had originally been named *HMS Northumberland*, a 5 masted ironclad frigate when she was launched in 1866. By 1904, she was obsolete but had been refitted as a training ship and renamed Acheron. She was moored at the Nore, where the River Thames meets the North Sea (just off Shoeburyness).

In February 1907, Harry was posted to **HMS Bulwark** for 18 months. Having just completed a refit, *Bulwark* joined the Channel Fleet but a series of accidents meant she spent the next 2 years being repaired at Chatham. Presumably this gave William the opportunity to spend time with Flo as his son Joe was born in 1908.

HMS Bulwark was not a lucky ship. In 1914, there was an explosion while she was moored at Sheerness and all hands (741 men) were lost. The court of enquiry concluded it had been caused when cordite ignited and the fire had spread to the aft magazine, which exploded, destroying the ship. Only 30 bodies were ever recovered.

In August 1908, Harry was posted to **HMS Duncan**, a pre-dreadnaught battleship. HMS *Duncan* initially went to Canada and was then assigned to the Mediterranean Fleet.

After leaving *HMS Duncan*, Harry was posted to a depot ship in Malta until a new posting arrived.

The most notable event whilst Harry was serving on *HMS Duncan* was the earthquake in December 1908, during which an estimated 70,000 people died. HMS Duncan was sent to Messina help with the relief operations and Harry's service record notes the award of a commemorative medal to all those involved.

65

A Brief & Incomplete Family History

It is interesting to note that some of the dates in Harry's service record do not match with the records of the ships movements. For instance, although Harry is recorded on the depot ship in Malta on 18 March 1909, his next ship on 19 March was actually in England. We can only assume that Marines transferring between ships would nominally remain on their old vessel's books making it impossible to identify travelling time between postings.

Harry joined **HMS Goliath** in March 1909 but the prop shaft broke during her initial voyage and she ended up back at Portsmouth for repairs. Harry returned to Chatham to await his next posting.

HMS Goliath was a pre-dreadnaught battleship launched in 1898. At the start of the First World War, she was assigned to the Dardanelles campaign. In May 1915, a Turkish destroyer slipped past patrols and torpedoed Goliath. Some 570 men, out of a crew of 750, were killed in the sinking.

By June, Harry was assigned to **HMS Vengeance** after she was damaged in a collision with a merchant ship at Portsmouth. He stayed with Vengeance until the end of July, when he returned to Chatham.

HMS Vengeance served in the Dardanelles in 1915 and later was involved in the capture of Dar es Salaam in 1916.

On 19th August 1909, Harry joined **HMS Black Prince**. She was a 12,600 ton armoured cruiser, launched in 1904, with 6 x 9" guns and 10 x 6" guns. Whilst Harry was on board, she was part of the Atlantic Fleet and was based at the Nore, so it was convenient to have his shore leaves at home in the East End of London. In all, Harry was on board Black Prince for 3 years. During this time he re-enlisted for another ten years service with the RMLI.

HMS Black Prince was sunk in 1916 during the Battle of Jutland. Black Prince lost contact with the rest of the Grand Fleet during the night, and found herself surrounded by German vessels and illuminated by searchlights. At point blank range, the Germans opened fire and Black Prince sank within 15 minutes with the loss of the entire crew of 857.

Harry had served on *Black Prince* for three years and had only left a few months before the battle. He must have served with most of the men who died.

After almost a year at Chatham, Harry was posted to **HMS Cressy** for 6 weeks in 1913. Considering what happened the following year, Harry can consider himself lucky it was such a short posting.

In September 1914, HMS Cressy was on patrol with her sisters, Aboukir and Hogue in the North Sea. Aboukir was struck by a torpedo and as Hogue approached her sinking sister, was torpedoed as well. Cressy attempted to ram the U boat but did not succeed, and as she attempted to pick up survivors from the first two ships, was also torpedoed. 62 officers and 1,397 enlisted men were lost from the 3 ships.

For the next year, and during the early stages of World War One, Harry was based at **HMS Ganges**. Although Ganges was later a shore based training establishment, at the time a number of different vessels were used for training and accommodation, mostly for young sailors. What Harry's role was at this time is not recorded.

In November 1915, Harry was posted to **HMS Champion**. By this stage, he must have been one of the oldest Marines on board and appears to have been given light (domestic) duties on board. Presumably this would have involved acting as Mess Servant for the officers. Traditionally, whilst the sailors man the A, B and Y turrets in battleships, the Marines man the X turret. But this is hard physical work in confined spaces and at nearly 40 years old it may have been too strenuous for a man with a slight physical frame.

HMS Champion was assigned to the Grand Fleet and was the leader of the 13th Destroyer Flotilla. She was a C-class light cruiser, with a displacement of 3,750 tons and 4 x 6" guns. She was based first at Scapa Flow in the Orkney Islands and later at Rosyth on the Firth of Forth (so we can assume Harry didn't get many shore leaves).

HMS Champion took part in the biggest fleet action of the First World War – the Battle of Jutland – in June 1916. Harry's name is on the crew list on the days of the battle so we know he was involved. Despite being in the thick of the action, there were no injuries on board.

The war ended on 11th November 1918 but he was not demobilized from HMS Champion until 23rd May 1919.

A Brief & Incomplete Family History

It is interesting to reflect on the changes that Harry saw in his lifetime.

DATE	NOTABLE EVENT	AGE
1876	Born in Bethnal Green	
1877	Victoria proclaimed Empress of India	1
1878	First phone call in USA	2
1879	Battle of Rorkes Drift	3
1881	Natural History Museum opens	5
1881	Living at 200, Old Ford Road	5
1883	First electric trams running in London	7
1884	Women first permitted at Oxford	8
1888	Jack the Rippers first victim	12
1891	Living at 10, Lyte Street, Bethnal Green (Tinker)	15
1895	First cars in UK	19
1896	First experimental radio message	20
1898	Joined the Royal Marine Light Infantry	22
1899	Boer War starts-William arrives 31st December 1899	23
1901	Queen Victoria dies	25
1903	First Wright brothers flight	27
1904	Married Florence on Christmas Day at St Leonards,	28
1908	White City stadium opened	32
1909	First old age pension paid	33
1909	Bleriot flight across the Channel	33
1909	William re-enlists in RMLI	33
1910	Edward VII is King	34
1912	Scott reaches the South Pole	36
1912	Titanic sinks	36
1914	Start of World War I	38
1916	Battle of Jutland	40
1918	Women get the vote (but only if over 30)	42
1919	Demobilised from RMLI	43
1920	Moves to Clydach South Wales with family	44
1926	First transatlantic phone call	50
1926	General strike	50
1927	First automatic traffic lights	51
1936	King George V is King	60
1936	BBC Television begins broadcasting	60
1938	Chamberlain & Hitler sign the Munich Agreement	62
1939	Start of WWII	63
1940	Died in South Wales	64

Florence Stevenson (1880 - 1962)

Parents   *Joseph William George **POLAIN** and Maria Ann **Boxell***
Siblings   *Joseph (1872), Maria Ann, (1874), John Albert (1876), Esther (1878), Maud Emily (1882), Arthur Henry (1887), Ethal Lillian (1891) and Cecil Percival (1892)*

Florence was born on 23rd April 1880 in Bethnal Green.

In 1881, the Census shows the family living at 27, Warner Place with Florence being aged 1. By 1891, the family had moved across the road to 18, Warner Place.

She went to Teesdale Street Infants School between 1886 and 1888, then moved to the senior School until 1892. When she was 13, the School Board issued a labour certificate giving her a total exemption from future attendance . The law required a minimum of 5 years study for children with a minimum of 250 attendances a year. The labour certificate would have allowed Florence to work full time, rather than attend school.

The 1901 Census return shows Florence, who was 21 at the time, still living at 18, Warner Place and her employment as a Boot Machinist. For many years she worked for I. Solomon and Co. but the factory closed in 1906. Her reference notes her as being of "good character".

She married Harry at St. Leonard Church, Shoreditch on Christmas Day 1904.

Her father was shown on the Marriage Certificate as deceased but he had been a Boot Maker.

Harry's father's job as Cabinet Maker is shown on the Marriage Certificate but it only has the 'mark' of his mother, suggesting Emily was illiterate.

At the time of the marriage, Florence was 24 and Harry was 28, and both were resident at 16, Great Cambridge Street.

We know that at some time after 1906, Florence moved to 6, Grove Road, Chatham as we have a character reference that the local priest gave her in 1909. We can assume that she moved to be closer to the RMLI barracks in Chatham where Harry was based.

When Harry re-enlisted in 1909, Flo was still living in Chatham.

A Brief & Incomplete Family History

Before 1915, Flo moved back to London and was living at 102, Old Bethnal Green Road. We think this was the house where her mother, Maria Polain was living, with her sister Ethel Lillian.

The war finished on 11 November 1918 and Private W.H. Stevenson (Service Number 10342) was demobilised from the Chatham Division of the RMLI on the 8th July 1919.

The period immediately following the end of the Great War was a difficult time. Millions of men had returned from the war to find no ready employment and great hardship. For Harry it must have been even more difficult as he had 20 years service in the military but had no trade to fall back on.

As far as potential employers were concerned he was unskilled and could only work as a labourer.

Harry went to work for the retired Engineering Commander of HMS Champion as a handyman at Wroughton House, Swindon in 1919 (presumably as an act of charity by his old boss). He then joined Florence at 102, Old Bethnal Green Road, where her sister and brother in law were already living.

The following year he found work with Great Western Railways but had to move to South Wales, away from all their friends and family. They moved to 19, Tanyrallt Road, Clydach, South Wales, just north of Swansea.

Harry died in 1940 at home in Clydach. He was 64 and had been retired for 2 years. He was buried at St. Johns Church in Clydach.

Florence died at home on 6th July 1962 aged 82. She was buried at St. Johns Church in Clydach.

A Brief & Incomplete Family History

It is interesting to reflect on the changes that Florence saw in her lifetime.

DATE	NOTABLE EVENT	AGE
1880	Born in Bethnal Green	
1881	Living at 27, Warner Place, Bethnal Green	1
1882	Married women can own property	2
1884	Women first play tennis at Wimbledon	4
1888	Women allowed the vote in county and borough elections	8
1891	Living at 18, Warner Place, Bethnal Green	11
1894	Women allowed to vote for parish councils	14
1901	Living at 18, Warner Place, Bethnal Green	21
1904	Married William at St Leonards Church, Shoreditch	24
1906	William Henry born	26
1908	Joseph born	28
1908	First woman Mayor	28
1914	First policewoman	34
1915	Violet Ivy born	35
1918	Women over 30 can vote if they own property	38
1919	Women can be Barristers, Solicitors and Accountants	39
1919	Nancy Astor first woman MP to sit in the House of Commons	39
1928	All women over 21 allowed to vote-the same as men	48
1958	First woman judge	78
1962	Died in South Wales	82

However, she would have had to have lived another 18 years for the Equal Pay Act, 23 years for the Sex Discrimination Act and 27 years to see the first woman Prime Minister in the UK.

William & Florence's children

Florence and Harry had three children;

- **William** (Billy) was born in 1906
- **Joseph** (Joe) was born in 1908
- **Violet Ivy** (Vi) was born in 1915. Vi was my mother and we look at her life in a little more detail below

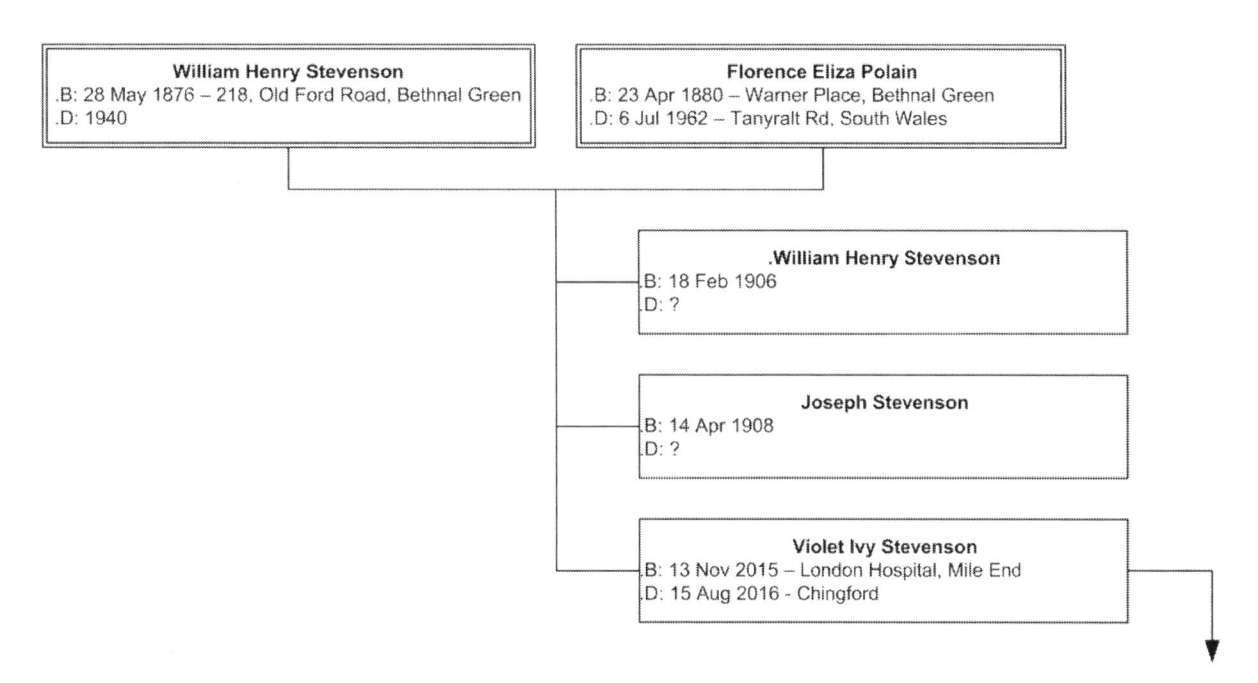

```
William Henry Stevenson                    Florence Eliza Polain
B: 28 May 1876 – 218, Old Ford Road,       B: 23 Apr 1880 – Warner Place, Bethnal Green
   Bethnal Green                           D: 6 Jul 1962 – Tanyralt Rd, South Wales
D: 1940

        ├──────── William Henry Stevenson
        │         B: 18 Feb 1906
        │         D: ?
        │
        ├──────── Joseph Stevenson
        │         B: 14 Apr 1908
        │         D: ?
        │
        └──────── Violet Ivy Stevenson
                  B: 13 Nov 2015 – London Hospital, Mile End
                  D: 15 Aug 2016 - Chingford
```

William Henry's family

7 PARENTS

William Alfred Polain (1912 - 1991)

Parents   *John Albert **Polain** and Jane **Holloway***
Siblings   *Jane (1897), John, (1898), Violet May (1904), Thomas Arthur (1905), Alice (1909)*

Bill was born on 25th April 1912 and the birth was registered at 42, Haroldstone Road. He was the baby of the family having 5 elder brothers and sisters. Bill was to live at that house for the next 68 years.

His school report from Coppermill Road Boys' School in 1926 says *"a boy of excellent disposition and very good abilities, who is doing really good work"*. He got "*Very Good*" for each subject and his conduct was noted as excellent.

Bill was a keen sportsman and played football and cricket for local teams. By trade he was a bricklayer, but as with all building trades he could turn his hand to most things.

Although Bill lived in Walthamstow and Violet lived in Bethnal Green, he obviously knew her through their family connection. They were certainly a 'couple' in 1936 as the photographs of them in Wales show.

In 1938, Bill and Violet were married at St. Michaels and all Angels, Walthamstow.

A Brief & Incomplete Family History

In 1938, Bill and Violet were married at St. Michaels and all Angels, Walthamstow.

With the world at war, it was inevitable that Bill would get called up into the military. In December 1941, he passed his National Service medical board exam, and being classed A1 was deemed fit for service. In the following June he was instructed to proceed to Blackpool, where he joined the 227th Training Regiment, Royal Artillery.

For the next three months, Bill underwent basic army training in Blackpool but clearly had some time to enjoy himself as Violet went to visit him in Blackpool when he had leave.

A Brief & Incomplete Family History

On completion of basic training, he was posted to Battery 462 of the Hertfordshire Yeomanry (the 86th Field Regiment) at Hovingham, Yorkshire. Almost immediately he was sent on training courses at Ironbridge in Shropshire. A new unit, formed out of parts of existing regiments, was formed in December 1942 and Bill was assigned to the new regiment, the Herts and Essex Yeomanry (191st Field Regiment, RA). As this regiment used different equipment and had a different role to his old regiment, he was again sent on specialist training courses at Shaftsbury, finally returning to his regiment is September 1943. The following 9 months were spent training for the invasion of Europe at a variety of locations, including Sutton, Wanstead and Snaresbrook, so home wasn't that far away. His regiment was assigned to support the Canadian 3rd Infantry Division in the forthcoming invasion.

On the 6th June 1944, Bill was embarked at 6 p.m. at the Royal Albert Docks as part of the invasion force. After a 3 day voyage on a troop ship and landing craft he landed on JUNO (Mike Beach), near Graye sur Mer to support the Canadian troops and British Royal Marine Commandos who were already ashore.

Many years later I watched the film "The Longest Day" with him, and he clearly remembered the Beach Master on Juno Beach.

Bill was a technical specialist in the mobile Forward Observation Posts for his battery, targeting the guns and reporting the fall of shot. The guns were 25 pounders, which were small and mobile, so they were always operating close to the front line.

Bill's battery was involved in the fighting around Caen in the weeks immediately following the invasion, and then travelled north east along the coast, taking part in the siege of Le Havre in September. From there his battery moved on as part of the 49th Division to Dieppe and Dunkirk, arriving in Turnhout by the 8th October. The Canadian push along the coast continued and they reached Antwerp by 14 October and Roosendaal (Holland) by early November, where the regiment paused to regroup.

Due to changing needs for manpower, the Herts and Essex Yeomanry was disbanded in November 1944, and Bill was sent home for leave for 2 weeks. Most of the men in the Regiment were sent to Infantry units but as Bill was a technical specialist he was re-assigned to the 1st Heavy Regiment, who were equipped with 6" and 7.5" artillery.

On the 24th February 1945, 8 months after the start of the fighting in France, Bill was wounded by German artillery fire after taking shelter in a barn. He was taken to the Regimental first aid post but was evacuated to the British 30 Brigade General Hospital in Lille for treatment. He was in the hospital for a month but after convalescence and some additional training (and a promotion) he returned to duty with the 1st Heavy Regiment in Holland on the 8th April 1945.

Even though the German Army surrendered in May 1945, Bill wasn't demobilised from the Army for 7 months and only returned back to the UK in December 1945. In the meantime he was stationed in Holland.

On his return to the UK, Bill found employment as a Bricklayer with the Metropolitan Water Board, and stayed with them for many years. However, as he got older the work and travelling became too demanding for him. He was also diagnosed with TB and spent 6 months in an isolation ward at Whipps Cross Hospital.

Sometime later he retired from the Water Board and found work as a security guard at the Wallace Collection in central London. He finally retired in 1977 on his 65th birthday.

The move to the new house in Richmond Road, Chingford in 1980 kept Bill busy for some time but he suffered a series of minor strokes over the years. Whilst he recovered well and he led an active life, a final stroke and pneumonia led to his death in Whipps Cross Hospital in 1991.

Bill was cremated at Enfield and his ashes were interred at St. Peter's and St. Paul's Church, North Chingford.

Violet Ivy Stevenson (1915-2016)

Parents   William Henry **Stevenson** and Florence Eliza **Stevenson**
Siblings   William Henry (1906), Joseph (1908)

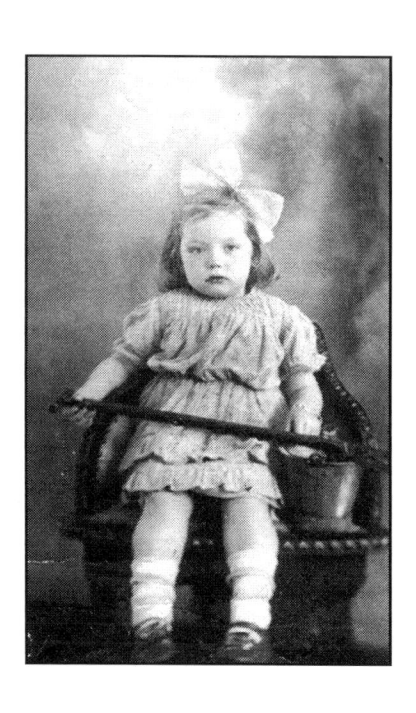

Violet was born in the London Hospital, Mile End Road on 13th November 1915.

Her mother registered the birth at 102, Old Bethnal Green Road and it is probable that Florence, Bill and Joe were living there after moving back from Chatham. Her family moved to Wales about 1920 to find work.

The period immediately following the Great War was a time of economic uncertainty. Prospects for her father after a lifetime in the Royal Marines must have been limited, especially after the demobilisation of the Army and Navy and the huge numbers returning to civilian life and looking for work.

Violet went to school in Wales and had vivid memories of growing up there. She left school at 14 but by then the Depression had started and the only work she could have found in Wales would have been in domestic service (as a maid or servant) or working in a shop.

It was decided her best opportunities lay in London and she returned to Bethnal Green to live with her grandmother, Maria. She never mentioned her grandfather as he had died many years before.

The East End of London she came back to would probably have been familiar to Charles Dickens and William Booth. The widespread destruction of the East End by German bombers and Town Planners wouldn't start for another 10 years. Whilst London's suburbs had expanded considerably over the previous 20 or 30 years, large areas of Bethnal Green, Shoreditch and Hackney would have been unchanged since Victorian times, just more decrepit and decayed. It was into this landscape that a 15 year old Violet started her working life, alone.

Having little in the way of skills to offer, she worked in a succession of poorly paid, unskilled jobs, but by about 1935 she was working as a shoe machinist in an East End factory. Over time she grew closer to her cousin Bill, and the friendship developed into love.

She married Bill at St. Michael's Church, Walthamstow on 3rd July 1938, and moved into a flat in the same house in Walthamstow where Bill's mother and father lived. Bill's mother died in 1939 before war broke out but John, Bill's father, continued to live at the same address.

At some point after the war, Bill and Vi bought the house from the landlord and carried on living there, and Bill's father moved to a flat near the High Street in Walthamstow.

Whilst her children were growing up, Violet worked in a series of clerical jobs in the City. She worked at Buckmasters and More (a stockbroker now owned by Credit Suisse) and at the Seed Trade Association near to Bunhill Row and the Wesley chapel.

In 1980, Vi and Bill sold the house in Haroldstone Road, Walthamstow and moved to Richmond Road in Chingford, E4. Vi continued to live at this address for the rest of her life. After a period of declining health brought on by a stroke, Bill died in 1991.

Violet died in Gracewell Nursing Home, Chingford, following a short illness at the age of 100. She was cremated at Hainault and her ashes were interred in Epping Forest at the Green Acres cemetery at North Weald.

Vi and Bill's children

William Alfred married Violet Ivy Stevenson in 1938. They had two children;

- **Brenda Ann** was born in 1946 and married Alan Dear in 1966. They had three children;

    - **Louisa** married Gary in 1999 and they had three children, Rebekah, Christopher and Matthew

    - **Liane** married John in 1997 and they had two children, Samuel and Nathan.

    - **Matthew** married Paula in 2005 and they had two children, Thomas and Lily May

- **Alan Robert** was born in 1950.

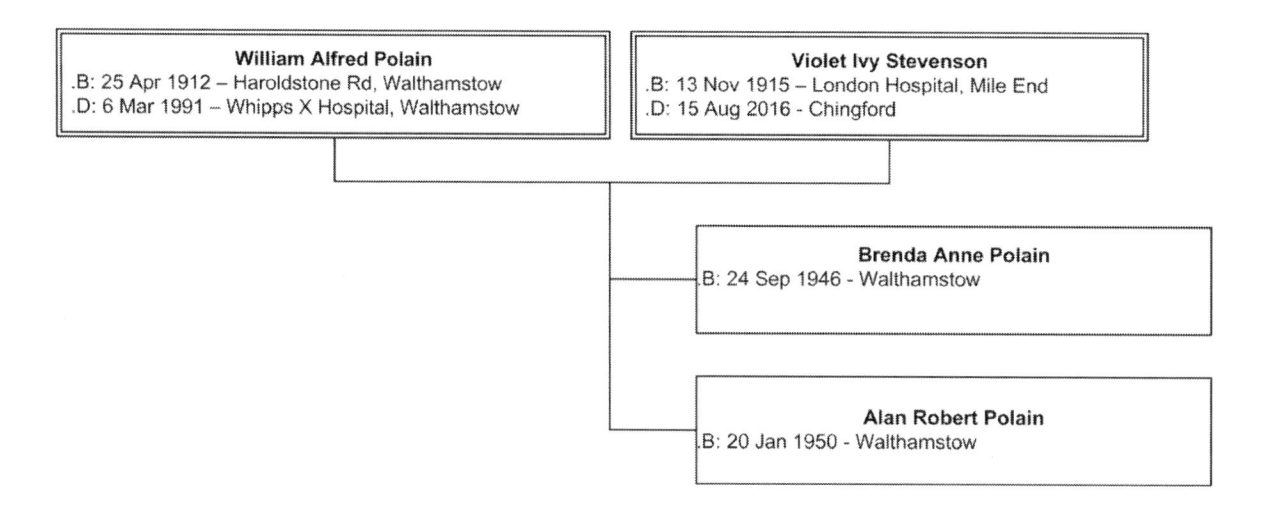

```
William Alfred Polain
B: 25 Apr 1912 – Haroldstone Rd, Walthamstow
D: 6 Mar 1991 – Whipps X Hospital, Walthamstow

Violet Ivy Stevenson
B: 13 Nov 1915 – London Hospital, Mile End
D: 15 Aug 2016 - Chingford

    Brenda Anne Polain
    B: 24 Sep 1946 - Walthamstow

    Alan Robert Polain
    B: 20 Jan 1950 - Walthamstow
```

William and Violet's family

A Brief & Incomplete Family History

PART TWO – LOOSE ENDS

Crime & Punishment

Samuel Polain

Samuel is a bit of a problem in the 'family history' sense.

It is likely his parents were William and Elizabeth Polain (nee Shoard) but as usual the records do not match exactly and we don't know if he married or when he died. However, some of the bits we do know give a fascinating insight to a particular aspect of Victorian life.

In short, Samuel was a petty thief, was convicted and punished by **transportation**.

It is an irony that our lives are best documented if you fall foul of the authorities. Samuel is a very good example of this.

On the 17th September 1838, Samuel was tried at the Central Criminal Court (Old Bailey) for the charge of Larceny.

At the time Samuel was 28 (born 1808) and single. His occupation was recorded as 'Weaver' in some of the records but he had already served time in prison for Felony (unfortunately we don't have any details). We can therefore assume that he fell foul of the Victorian equivalent of 'three strikes and you are out' rule.

The transcript of the trial is reproduced below:

Charge:

> **SAMUEL POLAIN** *was indicted for stealing, on the 16th of August, 17 yards of corduroy, value 12s.; 14 yards of cotton cloth, value 6s.; 430 buttons, value 4s.; and 3 oz. weight of thread, value 8d.; the goods of William Kilby; and that he had been before convicted of felony.*

Transcript of Proceedings:

> *Accuser* **WILLIAM KILBY** *. I am a tailor, and live in Gibraltar-Walk, Bethnal-Green. On the 16th of August I was going along Sun-Street, and met the prisoner—I had known him previously, but had not seen him a great while—he said he was in great distress—I took him into a public-house, and gave him a pint of beer—we came out, and he offered to carry a bundle that I had, containing the articles stated—I allowed him—before we got to Church-Street I gave him 6d., to relieve him, as he told me a pitiable story—I then said, at the corner of Brick-Lane, that before we separated, we would have a pint of ale—I went into the public-house, and while I was giving the order, he was gone with the bundle—I have not seen it since—he was taken on the Saturday following.*

> ***Prisoner***   *How can you swear to me?*

Accuser   *I cannot be mistaken in a person I knew three years ago, and who walked so far with me—I have not the slightest doubt that he is the man.*

Prisoner   *I knew him about three years ago; and did not see him till he accused me of the robbery.*

THOMAS SPURGEON *(police-constable 175 G.) I went with the prosecutor, and found the prisoner—he denied ever having seen the prosecutor in his life before.*

JOSEPH COLLISON *(police-constable R 136.) I produce this certificate of the prisoner's former conviction, from Mr. Clark's office—(read)—the prisoner is the man who was convicted.*

GUILTY . Aged 28.— ***Transported for Seven Years.***

Some of the streets named in the trial are still there but of course the whole area has been rebuilt. Gibraltar Walk and Brick Lane are only about 200 yards from "the Nichol" where some of the family members are recorded as having lived at the time of the 1851 census.

The subtleties of the Victorian justice system are beyond me but crimes seem to be broken into two main categories, Larceny and Felony. Larceny is defined as the *"unlawful taking and carrying away the property of another person with the intent to permanently deprive them of its use"* and is usually regarded as a misdemeanor.

Quite how this was interpreted in 1838 is unclear as the explanation given on 'The Old Baileys' web site gives a number of different types of larceny including *"from the person"*, *"in a dwelling"*, *"by a servant"* and just plain *"theft"*. Where the theft may have involved violence such as theft from a person, a sentence of 10 or 14 years seems the norm, but it appears that sheep stealing was a particularly horrid crime as that carried a 15 year sentence.

It is also confusing as to whether there was any distinction between *"larceny from a dwelling"*, *"housebreaking"* or *"burglary"*.

The charge of Felony was apparently reserved for more serious crimes such as murder. The Court records list Samuel's offence as *"Larceny before, convicted of Felony"*.

The police records include Sam's physical description:

Hair	Light	**Height**	5' 0½"
Eyes	Hazel	**Read & write**	Both
Complexion	Fresh	**Occupation**	Silk Dyer
Visage	Round	**Other** ….	
Make	Small	Slightly pock marked, scar on right arm, "I-S-P" on left arm	

> **NOTE:**
>
> Puzzled by the reference to "I-S-P" in the description, I looked it up on the internet. In 2020 a tattoo site defined it as;
>
> *"I-S-P is a universal acronym, created to inform the masses that you don't have to conform to what people think. In doing so, you choose what the letters I-S-P means for you".*
>
> It would be interesting to know if this was the meaning in 1838.

Samuel was sentenced to 7 years transportation. At 28, Samuel was about the average age for transportation, but in the same month as he was convicted, men as old as 50, and as young as 16 were also transported.

From London, Samuel was taken to Chatham on 2nd October, where he was imprisoned in "Fortitude", a prison hulk moored on the mud of the River Medway. "Fortitude" was formally the HMS Cumberland, a 74 gun 3rd rate, launched in 1807. Prison hulks were old ships that were not fit to go to sea and were usually-navy vessels that had been taken over by the Home Office. The ordnance and masts/rigging were removed and the ships moored away from the harbour to prevent escapes.

On the 23rd March 1839, Samuel was put on board the "Boadicia" and transported to Bermuda to serve his sentence.

The majority of prisoners for transportation went to New South Wales. From contemporary records it appears that not all convicts transported to New South Wales suffered badly as some were taken on as domestic servants and farm labourers, their services being paid for by settlers. By comparison, Bermuda appears to have been a very tough punishment for all the men sent there.

In Bermuda there were three prison hulks (Coromandel, Dromedary and Antelope) holding about 1100 men at any one time. Samuel was on "Antelope" and would have worked either in the quarries or on the building the Naval Dockyard. The work was physically hard, the weather hot and humid and disease and pestilence was rife. Essentially the convicts were used as slaves, as by that time slavery had been stopped in the colonies.

Yellow fever was rife on the island and in 1843 there was a major outbreak. On the 19th August 1843, Samuel was admitted to the Naval Hospital in Bermuda, suffering from the symptoms of Yellow Fever. His medical notes read:

> *"This was a very similar case to the one just described but the heat of skin and headache were more severe-one bleeding was ordered-and the same treatment as the last case.   Discharged 1st September"*

The previous patient was prescribed a purge!

Numerous prison registers for the period in Bermuda still exist (FindmyPast.com). They show nothing of much significance, other than Samuel is generally recorded as being in good health and of good behaviour. However, one Register shows 5 of the 25 prisoners on the page as having died in August. Overall, I estimate that about 30% of the prisoners died during captivity whilst Samuel was in custody, with another 10% being repatriated to England due to their poor health.

Samuel was returned to England on board the "Nautilus" on the 7th June 1845, and was transferred to the prison hulk "York" at Gosport. He was given a free pardon on the 4th July 1845 on completion of his sentence and released to return home.

Following his release, there are no further records of Samuel, even though registration of marriages and deaths became compulsory after 1837. So, after years of his life being meticulously documented by police, courts and the prison authorities, he disappeared without trace.

Samuel's pardon

* * *

Eliza Polain

Further down the range of misdemeanors, Eliza had a brush with the law in 1874.

Eliza and her husband James William (aged 27 and a Gasfitter) were arrested on the 3rd June and bailed on the 4th to appear at the at the Police Court in Worship Street (similar to Magistrate Court today) on the 11th June on the following charge:

> *"For that they, having contracted to provide sufficient food and other necessaries for an infant of Tender years, named Elizabeth Coleman, unable to provide for itself, did unlawfully neglect to provide the said Infant with sufficient food, whereby its health was injured"*

James was found **Not Guilty** but Eliza was not so lucky.

She was found guilty and sentenced to 6 months without Hard Labour, at the House of Correction in Westminster. We have no idea who the child was, or any more of the back story, but this appears to have been the sole stain on Eliza's character.

* * *

Missing in Action

Albert Edward Polain

Albert Edward, son of Frederick and Sarah Polain of St. Lukes, London, died on the 28th September 1916 during the Battle of the Somme.

Before the war, he had lived as a lodger with his sister, Mary Ann, and her husband Ernest Fosh, at their home at 89, Pedro Street, Clapton Park. He gave his trade as a Brush Maker.

After the outbreak of war he enlisted into the British Army. Rifleman Albert Edward Polain (R/22943) was in 'D' Company of 2nd Battalion, King's Royal Rifle Corps (KRRC). The KRRC, together with 2nd Royal Sussex, 1st Loyal North Lancs & 1st Northants, made up the 2nd Brigade/1st Division.

The Battle of the Somme had been going on since 1st July 2016 and wasn't to end until November. In practice the Battle of the Somme wasn't one continuous action, but a multitude of smaller battles spread across the whole of the front. One of these smaller actions became known as the Battle of Morval (25-28th September 1916). The British objective was the capture of Combles, Lesboeufs and Gueudecourt from the German forces.

The 2nd Brigade/1st Division was on the front during this period and there were numerous assaults on the German lines. Reading the accounts it appears that each failed assault by the British was followed by another that would be equally disastrous. Albert was killed at some point during this period. He was 28.

His body was never identified. His name is carved on the memorial at Thiepval (Pier/face=13B), along with 70,000 other servicemen's names who died on the Somme and have no known resting place.

It is rather sad to see the Army records for Albert. The Register of Soldiers Effects says the

Army owed him £2 14s 6d, presumably in back pay. There was also a £3 War Gratuity.

£1 18s 2p was paid on 18th October 1919 to each of his beneficiaries-his sisters, Mary (Fosh) and Alice (Gollop) and to his Sister in Law (not named) who was guardian of his nephew.

A total of £5 14s 6d doesn't seem a lot for a life lost in service to the country.

Victor George Polain

Victor George Polain, RN, was a Telegrapher on the light cruiser HMS Dunedin (D93) when she was torpedoed and sunk on 24th November 1941. The German submarine that sunk her (U-124), was commanded by Johann Mohr.

Victor was the son of George John and Louie Polain of Lower Willingdon, Sussex. His name is amongst those of the RN personnel lost at sea and is engraved on the Portsmouth War Memorial.

I am including this story for several reasons;

- I feel that as he gave his life for his country, the least I can do here is to remember his name and sacrifice
- The story of the sinking of HMS Dunedin was for many years kept secret as it involved the breaking of the German Enigma codes

HMS Dunedin was a light cruiser that was completed just after the Great War had finished. Although having been in reserve for many years due to her age she was brought back into service at the start of the Second World War. In 1940 the ship was sent to Bermuda to patrol for enemy submarines attacking shipping in the Caribbean and had some success by stopping French blockade runners.

After a refit in the UK she was sent on convey duties on the Freetown-UK routes. In the aftermath of the sinking of the German battleship Bismarck, the cruiser was dispatched on 29 May to search for a German supply ship reported by the Enigma code-breakers of Bletchley Park as being somewhere in the area. After extensive searching in the central Atlantic, a Swordfish aircraft from a carrier spotted and attacked the German fleet oiler that had been sent out to refuel U-boats. The crew of HMS Dunedin boarded the tanker and sailed it back to Bermuda. Some important Enigma material was later found where it had fallen behind a filing cabinet in the wireless room.

In November 1941 the Admiralty learned from decrypted Enigma messages that a German armed merchant raider and supply ship was operating in the South Atlantic and ordered three cruisers to track them down independently.

On the same day, the 24th November, U-124, on her way to a rendezvous, sighted the unescorted **HMS Dunedin** steaming a zigzag pattern at 17 knots east of St. Paul's Rock. The U-boat raced ahead of the ship's path and dived for a submerged attack. The lookouts on the cruiser saw the periscope at 14.50 hours and changed course to chase the U-boat. The approaching U-124 suddenly came to the surface for a brief moment, but remained unseen. As Mohr was able to see through his periscope, he spotted a vessel at a range of over three miles, which was now well past of a favourable attack range. Mohr decided to fire a spread of three torpedoes at 15.21 hours. After 5 minutes and 23 seconds, two torpedoes struck the cruiser, which rolled first to port then to starboard before sinking stern first after 17 minutes.

The first torpedo struck amidships and wrecked the main wireless station. The second torpedo struck further aft, probably near the quarters of the officers; dismounting the after 6in gun and blowing away the starboard screw.

Out of the original crew of 486 officers and men, about 250 survivors managed to leave the ship by jumping overboard. They rescued themselves onto seven Carley floats and floating debris.

Many of them were wounded, and very little in the way of survival equipment had survived the sinking. Sharks were an obvious menace, but for men with open wounds and their skin softened by immersion in water for days, they were not the only killers.

The language of the official report submitted by Lt Commander Watson, the senior surviving officer, conveys some of the horror:

> "... an unknown type of small fish was extremely ferocious. They were less than a foot long and blunt nosed, quite unlike barracuda.
>
> "During the first and each successive night many men sustained deep bites from these fish. The bites were clean-cut and upwards of an inch or more deep, and were mostly in the soles of the feet, although in some cases the fish sprang out of the water and bit into the men's arms.
>
> "Frequently the bites resulted in severed arteries and many men died from this cause. The gratings and nettings of the rafts did not prevent the fish from attacking from inside the rafts."

Because the mission was secret and based on Enigma intercepts, no distress signal was sent.

Only 67 survivors were still alive on the six floats found by an American merchant ship three days after the sinking. Many survivors drowned, some died of their injuries, others died of exhaustion and some were bitten and killed by sharks.

A Brief & Incomplete Family History

There is a web site specifically for descendents and survivors of the Dunedin crew (The HMS Dunedin Society) which has a list of crew members when the ship was torpedoed.

His name is on the Portsmouth Naval Memorial (Panel 52, Column 3).

If you would like to find out more about this story, there is a book **BLOOD IN THE SEA- HMS Dunedin and the Enigma Code** by **Stuart Gill** available on Amazon.

* * *

"Polains" in the Middle Ages?

Introduction

In searching for the "Polain" name on the internet, a whole string of ancient Polains emerged. They had been included in a manuscript *"Miroir des Nobles de Hesbaye"* describing various family links in Belgium in the 13th to 15th century. The book was written by Jacques de Hemricourt (1303-1403), who was the Bishop of Liege and documents the nobility in the bishopric of Liege. The manuscript was published about 1450, and was subsequently published in the 17th century (containing a huge amount of speculation and assumptions) and again in the 19th century.

The manuscript was written in an ancient form of French and is impossible to understand unless you are a scholar specialising in this field. It is also not helped as in the 14th century, consistent spelling was the exception rather than the rule. I have found the following variations on the Polain family name spelling; Paulin, Poulain, Plain, Poul, Plaine, Pilan, Piland, Pollen and Pollain and there will be other variants I haven't found.

The version published in 1673 contained the original text as well as a translation, but modern scholars suggest that the translation is 'speculative'. The version published 1791 is little better, and it wasn't until 1920 that the Belgium Government published an updated version, with cross references to other available manuscripts. However, even this is difficult to translate into English (academics writing in French have a style that doesn't translate to English easily and Google Translate has its limitations).

Even the latest versions are nearly 500 pages long and how the 'List of Contents' work is still a mystery to me. However, the latest version contains family trees for all the noble families in Hesbaye and it is clear that the "Polain"s (or variants such as Guillaume Le Polain de Waroux and le Polain d'Alleur) married into numerous noble families in the area.

I found it difficult to work through the family histories as there is no consistency. Family names were not always stated in the text, so it was impossible for me to understand if William of Waroux is the same person as William Polain of Waroux.

The term 'knight' was at this time a job description, rather than a heraldic title for nobility. Sons could change their allegiance and coat of arms, in some cases reverting to titles and coats of arms of their ancestors. Titles such as 'Duke' referred to the number of knights and troops a noble could supply to the King, so titles would cease and not be passed from father to son. Titles didn't mean there was any direct connection to specific towns or lands, and ownership of the land didn't necessarily mean that the associated title was linked to it.

To confuse issues even more, the Bishop of Liege when describing the marriages and relationships between individuals didn't bother to note the date of birth and only occasionally a marriage date or date of death. They seem to have been a fertile bunch in the Middle Ages even if life was frequently short. Two, three or four wives seemed commonplace (Agnes was a very popular name), and large numbers of children (few of whom survived to adulthood). These factors make it impossible to know whether the text is referring to father, son or grandson.

It was only later in the Middle Ages that titles for nobility became linked to fixed estates and became hereditary.

The Index of *"Miroir Des Nobles De Hesbaye"* lists at least eleven different Jean le Polain, but it isn't clear how they were related. If time permits, I should find a family historian in Belgium that can filter thru the available documents and see if there are any conclusions to be found.

Ironically, in addition to the author of "Miroir", two people have written books about the history of Liege. One was Jacques de Hemricourt, obviously a descendent of the original author 600 years before, and Matthieu Lambert Polain. The names Hemricourt and Polain both feature heavily as being noble families in the Liege area in the original manuscript. Both men wrote their books in the 1800s and they were published by the Belgium Government.

Clearly it is unrealistic to assume there is any connection between these Polains of Waroux and the parents of Claude, nearly 400 years later. Liege is 180km away, but that isn't so far to travel over 200 years. Ancestory.com list a few records for Le Polain and Polain families in northern France, but nothing that looks as if there is any direct connection between the ancient Polains and the modern tribe.

Despite the separation in time, class and distance between the Polains of Waroux and Claude's parents in Templeux-le-Guerard, reading up on the wars opens up a window on a world that is, to modern eyes, totally alien and incomprehensible.

Part of the "Miroir" was a description of a war between the families of Waroux and Awans, which is detailed below.

The storm clouds gather

The war between Waroux and Awans was really a private quarrel between two rich and powerful families. The story is long and complex and includes murder, assassination, suffocation, single combat, beheadings, arson, ransom, treaties, truces, looting, pitched battles and treachery, even drawing the Pope in Rome into the dispute.

In most senses, the 'war' resembled a Corsican family feud. Every 'tit' generated a responsive 'tat' from the other side. Aggressive actions escalated over time, neighbouring families were drawn in, families linked by marriage became embroiled, rich people in the towns were forced to take sides. The warfare wasn't continuous but erupted every few years, as passions were raised and tempers were frayed.

The 'war', which lasted more than 30 years, was documented principally by Jacques de Hemricourt, the Bishop of Liege, as an extension of his history of the nobility of the Liege area.

Waroux and Awans were two small towns just to the east of Liege. If the location of the present day towns of the same name is any guide, they are only about 5 kilometres apart (they are near the present runway at Liege airport). We have no record of how big the towns were in the 13th century, but it appears that the whole district was filled with large, thriving communities so Waroux and Awans would not have been exceptional.

The area around Liege has a unique history. After the fall of the Roman Empire, Franks from Germany invaded southern Holland and the area we now know as Belgium. It was a prosperous area, made rich by the production and export of woollen cloth to England and the rest of the Continent. There were a number of 'city states' that stood out, including Liege and Aachen, where Charlemagne ruled an empire that stretched from Scandinavia to the Mediterranean.

After Charlemagne's death, his empire receded south, leaving the bishopric of Liege an isolated outpost of the Christian Holy Roman Empire from the 9th century until the 19th century, ruled by the Bishop of Liege on behalf of the Pope.

Private wars were not uncommon in the Middle Ages. Since the 9th century, "Charlemagne's Law" guaranteed nobility immunity in the law of the common people. In addition, the love of war was at that time one of the dominant passions of noble families. The slightest insult served as a pretext for a recourse to arms.

The Bishop was not an idle bystander of events, as he was the largest landowner in the area, as well as setting the laws, the judge, civil administrator and military commander of the church's militia. He had two historical rights-if a truce between battles was called, he would determine the conditions of the armistice and how long it would be. If anyone transgressed, he would sentence them to death. The church also had the sole right to destroy property by arson and to sentencing people to death by fire.

The Polains were linked to many of the families in Liege by marriage and would have inevitably been drawn into the conflict. But the only direct evidence we have of their involvement was the death of Jean le Polain, a knight, at the Battle of Donmartin, in 1325.

Considering how well documented the names of all the participants were, it is surprising that this is the only record of our involvement.

Presumably, Polains in the 13th century were good at keeping their heads down and avoiding involvement

However, even without evidence of the Polain family being directly involved in the war, the story is worth recounting in some detail for the light it shines on a part of history that we, as modern day observers, will never really understand.

The War starts

In 1297, a quarrel erupted between Humbert Corbeau, the Lord of Awans and Guillaume, the Lord of Waroux. They were the two most powerful families in the district of Hesbaye.

Humbert, who believed himself to be superior to his neighbours, decided to marry Adele, a young servant, to his cousin. Although she was of low birth, she was rich in furniture and inheritances and the Lords of the manor assumed the right of deciding who was to marry who, in order to keep the money within their clan.

Before the wedding she was abducted by Hanechon of Waroux and he married her. Humbert demanded her return to Awans, to compensate for his loss of face. Guillaume replied that she was free so that she could marry whom she liked.

Both sides sought support from their relatives, making 'blood bonds' (quite literally, drinking each other's blood to cement the agreements). The Awans decided to settle the dispute by force and invaded the Waroux lands, looting castles, houses, killing the livestock and burning the mill and breweries.

Feudal laws derived from ancient Saxon laws defined the feth as a private conflict among noble lineages. In a feth, every nobleman was expected to avenge his relatives or allies killed during the conflict. Accordingly, the noble families allied to the Awans and the Waroux were dragged into the struggle, which turned into a bloody vendetta.

The Lord of Awans was killed in 1298, which paradoxically strengthened his side, since all the members of his lineage had to join the vendetta. Due to the complicated genealogic links, different members of the same family joined the two opposed parties. It was decided that each battle would be followed by a 40 day truce in order to sort the genealogical mess and to allow every noble to choose his party.

The Lord of Waroux besieged and set fire to a tower held by the supporters of the Awans. This upset the Bishop who held the exclusive right of arson. To punish the knights responsible they were made to crawl on hands and knees to the Cathedral in Liege as penitence.

The bishop of Liège attempted to stop the conflict but was suspected of supporting the

Waroux. The Awans presented themselves as the champions of the oppressed. The vendetta turned into a generalized conflict and spread all over the principality.

The Awans sent a party to Rome to petition the Pope. The bishop was excommunicated and the Pope transferred him to another city. He was replaced by Alphonse de la Marck (1313). La Marck was young and fearless, but inexperienced. He decided to get rid of the vendetta, the murders and the troubles which devastated his principality.

On one occasion, one of the Waroux party was murdered before the end of the truce agreed with the Bishop. The murderer clearly thought he had a good excuse, but the Bishop wouldn't accept his power being usurped, and had the knight beheaded.

Using his ancient right of arson, he ordered the demolition and burning of the houses belonging to known murderers and looters. Unfortunately, this was again perceived as support to the Waroux, who were already hated by the people in Leige. Upon pressure from the people of Liège, the bishop was forced to flee in 1315.

At one point, a challenge was issued for single combat in an arena in the centre of Liege (on a matter of honour after one of the families was accused of murder). One knight turned up at the appointed hour but the other, having been pre-warned by the Bishop, arrived much later. By the end of the morning, the first knight was exhausted from having to wait in the heat and in full amour. The second knight, known as 'the bastard Hognoul' arrived after noon, and after both had made their confessions to the priest, the fight commenced. Eventually after a long and bloody fight, with both men injured, Hognoul prevailed. The Aldermen of the city, who had been spectators to the duel, certified Hognoul the victor.

By now, the dispute involved families and towns across the whole district. There were raids on homes, buildings and warehouses, ambushes and beatings, and more raids in retaliation. This went on, intermittently, for many years with no one side gaining a particular advantage.

The Awans and the Waroux did not lay down their arms. After several non-conclusive skirmishes, they met on 25 August 1325 in the plains of Dommartin, near Huy. As both sides charged the other, the horse of the Lord of Waroux stumbled and fell. Immediately one of the Awans knights jumped to the ground and killed him with an axe, but was then killed himself. The 270 Awans knights, led by Guillaume de Waremme, defeated the 350 Waroux knights, led by Henry II de Hermalle. Over 60 knights were killed, including Jean le Polain de Waroux.

Two years later, the conflict between the people of Liège and the bishop resumed. The bishop, allied with the Counts of Gelderland and Berg, won a series of fights and the peace of Vottem was signed in 1331, but with Liege effectively under the control of the Aldermen.

Finally in 1335, after 38 years, the families of Waroux and Awans reached agreement at the Abbey of Saint Laurent, near Liege. The agreement forbad private wars and sentenced to banishment the noblemen taking part in a vendetta. At the end of the war, the son of the Lord of Awans, married the daughter of the Lord of Waroux and a church dedicated to the twelve apostles was built to honour the victims of the war.

There is no record of what happened to Hanechon and Adele, whose forbidden love was the source of the war.

The best description of the war I have found is the "LA GUERRE DES AWANS ET DES WAROUX" by Christophe Masson, published in the Belgium magazine *"The Middle Ages"*. There is a badly translated version of this article in my files, explaining the political and social background, but even this abbreviated account is about 60 pages long and not for the faint hearted as the Google translation is particularly tortured.

Present Day

The key locations are Waroux, Awans and Alleurs. The modern villages bearing those names are about 2-3km apart and only 7km from the centre of Liege. Today, they are the suburbs of Liege and form part of a continuous band of housing to the north of the city's airport. To the casual traveller, there is nothing that can be seen today that suggests the antiquity of the towns or their tragic past.

At Waroux, there is a small fortified house, now privately owned and called Chateau Waroux. The present building was built some time after the war in the Middle Ages.

However, there is a family link with the past. A Belgium family have been given the right to adopt the surname *'Le Polain de Waroux'*. I get the impression that this change in name is fairly recent. An internet search will find them.

According to a Belgium genealogical website, this title indicates the holder to be a Knight. I have also seen a reference in a list of ancient Belgium aristocracy to a Polain who was a Count in the late Middle Ages. However, in France and Belgium, I understand that titles such as Duke and Count were not associated with the land that was owned.

Quite how you can prove you are the direct descendent after 700 years is a mystery, especially when there may be many other claimants to the title. Maybe the burden of proof demanded isn't that great or maybe titles can still be bought in Belgium. I have asked in Belgium about our name and the title 'Chevalier' (Knight). They were not impressed and I got the impression from the locals that it wasn't taken too seriously and considered an affectation.

Possibly the name (and title) *'Le Polain d'Alleur'* is still available to anyone in the family who is interested?

A Brief & Incomplete Family History

PART THREE - REFERENCE

APPENDIX A

The 'Old Nichol'

In 1680 John Nichol of Gray's Inn, who had built seven houses in Bethnal Green, leased 4.75 acres of gardens for 180 years to a London mason, Jon Richardson, with permission to dig for bricks. The land became built up piecemeal with houses, built by a number of sub-lessees. Many of the streets were named after Nichol, and by 1827 the 5-acre estate consisted of 237 houses.

The **"Morning Chronicle"** reported in 1850 that:

> *"Roads were unmade, often mere alleys, houses small and without foundations, subdivided and often around unpaved courts. An almost total lack of drainage and sewerage was made worse by the ponds formed by the excavation of brick earth.*
>
> *Pigs and cows in back yards, noxious trades like boiling tripe, melting tallow, or preparing cat's meat, and slaughter houses, dust heaps, and 'lakes of putrefying night soil' added to the filth.*
>
> *The limits of a single article would be insufficient to give any detailed description of even a day's visit. There is nothing picturesque in such misery; it is but one painful and monotonous round of vice, filth, and poverty, huddled in dark cellars, ruined garrets, bare and blackened rooms, teeming with disease and death, and without the means, even if there were the inclination, for the most ordinary observations of decency or cleanliness".*

In 1861, the same author noted that the Nichol had grown even more squalid in the last 20 years as old houses decayed and traditional trades became masks for thieves and prostitutes. He also noted the numbers inhabiting unfit cellars, the lack of sanitation and that running water was only available for 10–12 minutes each day (excepting Sundays!)

That is not to say that the conditions people lived in within the old Nichol estate were exceptional, or that London slums were worse than in other parts of the country. It is possible, if not likely, that George's brothers, sisters and parents lived in similar conditions. What makes the Nichol exceptional is that the lives of ordinary people were so well documented for posterity.

Up to this point, the poor and destitute of England were helped by charity from the rich or by the local parish councils. There was no national solution to the problems of the unemployed and elderly, no Old Age Pension, no Unemployment Benefit. Lack of jobs and opportunity, minimal and irregular wages for those with some form of employment, sickness, poor and unsanitary living conditions pushed the residents of the Nichol estate towards crime and drink.

Early in Victoria's reign, the outcry about the conditions in the Nichol reached a national scandal. The estate came to represent the living conditions of the country's poor and destitute and gained huge notoriety and publicity. Newspapers sent undercover reporters to wander the streets, reporting on the lives of the people and the living conditions. There were studies of the buildings and the sanitation. There was a public outcry over slum landlords.

Life in the 'Nichol'

The houses were originally small and closely spaced. Based on the census returns, a room would serve as bedroom and kitchen for a family. There could be 4 families per 4 room house. As the rooms were so small, people would share a bed or sleep on the floor.

Over the years, as the slum landlords sought to get more profit from their investment, additional dwellings were built between the houses and in yards and any open space. Therefore the whole area became a maze and in some cases it was only possible to leave a building by a tunnel connecting two or more basements.

The streets were not generally paved and what pavement existed was in poor condition. There was no water supply to the houses. Water went to standpipes in courtyards (serving perhaps 30 to 50 families) and it was normal to get water only a few times a week, for two hours at a time. Therefore water had to be collected, stored and boiled before use.

There were privies, generally shared between a number of households, in the back yards or courts (basically a plank over a hole in the ground) with little privacy for users. The cess pits were expensive to clean out so frequently overflowed.

There was no electricity in those days and no gas to the houses. Light was provided in the rooms by candles or small oil lamps. Broken glass windows either remained broken or were boarded over.

People not only lived in the estate, but businesses were run from the dwellings. Houses had workshops either in the basement or in the roof; materials were shipped in and out and stored for use; cattle and horses were kept (and slaughtered) so the waste was animal as well as human.

Half Nichol Street

Half Nichol Street was included in the demolition of the Old Nichol district during the 1890s. However, from the available documents it is possible to describe it in some detail.

No. 21, where Elizabeth was recorded as living in 1851, was on the north side of the street and was built some years after the buildings on the south side of the road. The buildings on the south side of the street (i.e. the buildings with even numbers) were generally 3 storey's high (ground floor and 2 floors) but without basements. The buildings on the north side of the street were 2 storey, no basements, built from brick and with tiled roofs. The 2 storey buildings had 2 rooms on the 1st floor and 2 rooms on the ground floor. There would have been a privy behind the house, but no piped water or sinks in any of the houses. Likewise, in the 1850s, there was no gas piped into the houses so all lighting at night would have been by oil lamps. Houses had fireplaces, but due to the high price of coal, heating and cooking would generally be done over fires fueled by wood.

There was however, a public wash house for the cleaning of cloths. The fad for cleaning bodies didn't really take off until later, when Public Bathhouses (slipper baths) were built by the local authorities or rich benefactors. I can't see any evidence of one anywhere on the Old Nichol.

There were 2 small shops at 43 and 47, at the junction with Sarah Street and Nichol's Row. At number 49 (on the corner of Sarah Street) was the "Lord Nelson" pub. All the other buildings would have had either workshops or rooms at ground floor level.

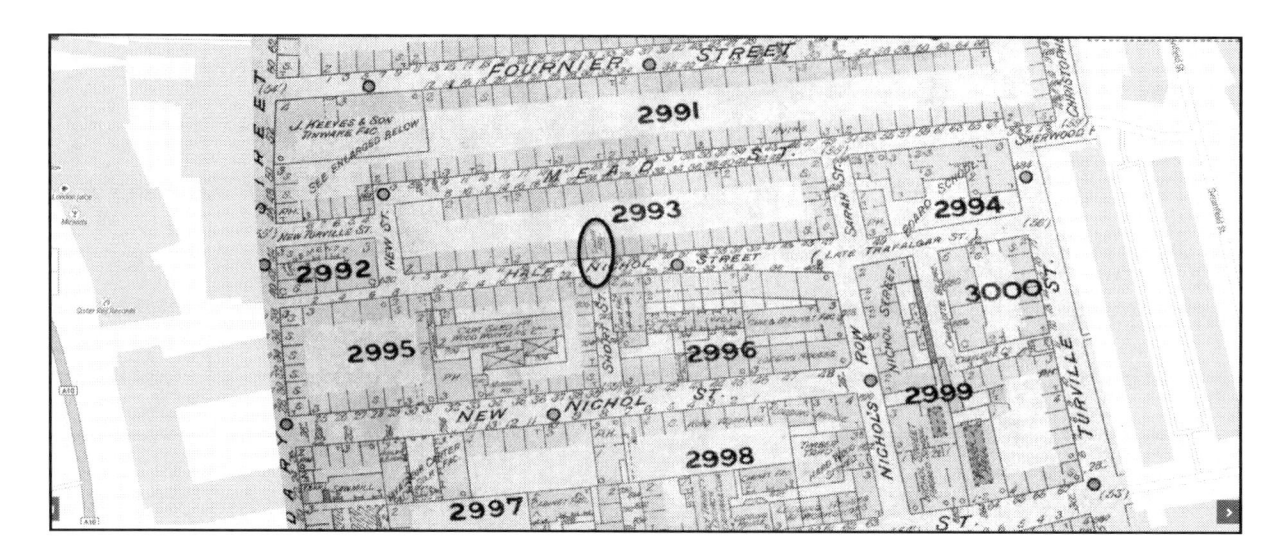

A detail from the Fire Insurance Survey maps of 1890 (British Library) showing Half Nichol Street, including house numbers. #21, where George and Elizabeth lived, is marked. Some of the family later lived in Trafalgar Street, an extension of Half Nichol Street.

The street itself had a paved footpath and a granite roadway. There was no rainwater drainage or sewers in the street. A review by the sanitary inspector described it as very dirty, with the gutters full. Between the south side of Half Nichol Street and New Nichol Street, and between New Nichol Street and Old Nichol Streets, the space at the back of the houses (where nowadays we would expect to see gardens) were filled with small workshops, courts, alleys etc. But the houses in Half Nichol Street backed onto the houses in Mead Street and there is no record of there being any industry behind the houses (the records of the insurance surveys from 1890 still survive). In this respect, Half Nichol Street may have been less of a warren than the rest of the Old Nichol.

As far as I can measure, Half Nichol Street would have been about 20 feet wide. This seems to be typical of the roads in the Nichol.

A study of the living conditions by Charles Booth, a well known social reformer, documented living conditions across London and made maps, colour coded to reflect the people living in specific streets. Half Nichol Street was categorised by Booth as **"lowest class, vicious, semi-criminal"** and *"Very poor, casual, chronic want"*.

Another article, published with the title ***"Ragged London"*** (see below) contains the following description:

> *"In Old Nichols Street, a turning in this district leading off from Shoreditch, we have a specimen of an east-end thieves' street. Its road is rotten with mud and water; its houses are black and repulsive; and at least fifty dark sinister faces look at you from behind blinds and dirty curtains as you pass up the rugged pavement."*

George and Elizabeth shared their house (number 21) with 3 other families. On the ground floor there was Benjamin Bryan with his wife and 5 children. Ben was a carpenter. In the back room, George Polain, Elizabeth and 4 children lived and probably worked on a hand loom. On the 1st floor were a family of 4 and another family of 5-a total of 21 people living and working in one house. Looking at contemporary photographs, if it was typical of the other 2 storey houses in the Nichol, we can assume it was one family to one room. That would have meant people sleeping head to toe on either a single bed or on the floor.

There was no separate kitchen but we know for sure there was a privy at the back of the house. We know this because the state of the yard of number 21 (where our ancestors lived) and the street itself is described in detail in ***"Sanitary Ramblings"*** (see below):

> ***"Half Nichol Street-***
>
> *On the surface of this street were bountifully strewn all kinds of dust, dirt, refuse, and garbage. It is not cleansed more than once in three weeks or a month; and though cleansed (nominally) only last week, it was as filthy and dirty as if apparently it had not been cleansed for months. This state of very many of the streets arises not only from the extreme want of accommodation for storing refuse till the dustman shall remove it, but from the dust contractor utterly neglecting to remove it. The inhabitants, therefore, in order to get rid of all their refuse, solid as well as fluid, are compelled to throw it on the streets, there to putrefy and be mixed up with the mud. In consequence of the free*

exposure of the animal and vegetable remains in a pasty state to the sun, the muddy compost becomes most offensive to the smell, and a constant cause of disease and death to the inhabitants. Invariably, wherever such filthy streets are found, so likewise are fever and the other zymotic diseases.

Loud complaints were made to me that the only way to get rid of the refuse was to throw it on the streets, as the dustmen would not take it away unless paid for so doing. The inhabitants of this street complained bitterly that "the people in it never died a natural death, but were murdered by the fever."

In the back yards of No. 21 in this street the soakage from the neighbouring privies had permeated through the wall, infiltrated it, and spread itself over the yard, where the offensive fetid soil was covered over, and as it were dammed up by collections of dust, cinders, and refuse. The poor-rate collector complained of this place as a great nuisance."

Life and Death in the Nichol

Considering his back yard was an open sewer, it is no surprise that George died of Cholera during the Third Asiatic Cholera pandemic. Cholera is an infectious disease with symptoms that include severe watery diarrhoea, which can lead to dehydration and death. It is caused by eating food or drinking contaminated water and is most common these days in places with poor sanitation, famine and overcrowding.

The biggest threats to life in 1850 were Typhus and Diarrhoea, which accounted for 70% of the deaths in the Nichol estate. Smallpox, Measles and Scarlet Fever accounted for most of the other deaths.

Due to the dampness of the buildings and the cramped conditions, illnesses of the chest such as consumption were rife. Cholera seems to have been accepted as a fact of life and a natural consequence of life in the poorer parts of town.

Whooping cough, scarlet fever, diphtheria, measles, smallpox, bronchitis and especially tuberculosis had a fatality rate in the Nichol that was twice as high as the surrounding area. While the contagion rate in the Nichol was not higher than elsewhere, inhabitants were less likely to recover.

Even in death there was no dignity. Burial grounds such as St. Matthews and Gibraltar Row were full and there were always complaints about the smell in warmer weather.

To put more bodies into the graveyards, soil was piled on top of the old burials so that the graveyards stood high above the surrounding streets.

The 'summer diarrhoea' that occurred annually and killed many, was largely caused by swarms of flies feeding on manure, rotting food and human waste in the hot, steaming streets.

Smell was a potent characteristic of London life. In the 1850s London experienced the Great Stink when the River Thames became a giant sewer overflowing not only with human waste but also dead animals, rotting food and toxic raw materials from the riverside factories.

"Sanitary Ramblings"

In 1848, Hector Gavin, a doctor, published his report for the 'Health of Towns Association'. It was titled **"Sanitary Ramblings-being Sketches and Illustrations of Bethnal Green"**, describing, in detail, the public health issues.

It mentions Half Nichol Street and the house that Elizabeth lived in, so I have included some excerpts from it (below) to show that even by the standards of the time, the conditions in the Old Nichol left a lot to be desired:

> ***"The District***
> *This district exceeds all those which have gone before it in filth, disease, mortality, poverty, and wretchedness; it abounds with the most foul courts, and is characterized by the prevalence of the greatest nuisances, and perennial foulness. Unlike the last district, there are several gardens in it resembling those already described, but infinitely surpassing them in everything degrading to our civilization. For many years this district has been notorious as the hot-bed of epidemics. This is easily explained, when the foulness of the streets, the dense crowding in some parts, and the nearly total absence of drainage and house-cleansing, are considered. The drainage, in fact, is characteristic of primitive barbarism; the drains are very near the surface, and some of the houses are built over them; the streets are perpetually covered with the most offensive fetid mud; the population is very dense, as many as 30 persons residing in a single house- 57 houses had a population of 580 persons. In about half a mile square of these houses and streets 30,000 persons are congregated;*

---- ++++ ----

> *The houses built by the French refugees are all several storied, and have large rooms on each floor, with a common staircase; the houses are, without exception, let out in rooms; each room contains a family, with a bed common to all; generally it is a work-room as well as a dwelling-room. Ventilation in these rooms is in the most defective state; the atmosphere is most oppressive, and loaded with unhealthy emanations; it is a common practice to retain the faecal remains in the rooms, in order to avoid exposure, and the perfect nastiness of, the common privies.*

---- ++++ ----

> *There are great numbers of low public-houses and beer-shops in this district; all these are*

crowded with lodgers, and thus become great nuisances, and sources of disease and immorality. Since several streets have been pulled down by the Railway Company, there has been much overcrowding; so much so, that not a habitation or lodging can be had in the neighbourhood, and some persons are, even now, in opposition to the law, residing in cellars, because they can find no place else to reside. The poor inhabitants generally prefer any kind of abode to the workhouse.

The occupations of the inhabitants are chiefly weaving and shoe-making; hawkers, toy-makers, and cabinet-makers, abound here, and the women wind silk and cotton. Those small manufactures which are carried on here are chiefly prepared in the prospect of being sold to the ready-money shops, or on speculation. The earnings of the population of this district are very low and precarious,

---- ++++ ----

Their common food consists of potatoes and bread, and butcher's meat of a very inferior quality. Numerous chandlers' shops are in the habit of supplying this inferior kind of food, and of receiving goods as pledges for its payment; these pledges are sold at the end of a month, if unredeemed.

---- ++++ ----

Moral debasement and physical decay, naturally enough, accompany the utter defiance of all the laws of health, and the complete disregard of all the characteristics of civilization. Such a population always supply our courts with criminals, our gaols with convicts, our charities with paupers, and our hospitals with the sick and diseased; and impoverish the honest, labouring poor, by the heavy poor-rates to which they give rise.

"Dwelling Houses"

It is lamentable to observe, in this extensive and populous parish, the enormous number of dwellings which have been constructed in defiance of every law and principle on which the health and lives of the occupants depend. In a vast number of instances, the dwellings have been planted, or stuck on the ground, with scarcely any foundation; great numbers have the clay, or damp ground, immediately below the wooden floors; they are very often below the level of the front or back-yards, or streets-from the first cause the rooms are excessively damp, and, in an extraordinary number of instances, truly uninhabitable; from the second cause, they are liable to be flooded, either on the occurrence of showers of rain, or when the water-pipes are left running. The dwellings are, in innumerable instances, considerably below the level of the whole of the surrounding neighbourhood, and are thus rendered very damp, as well as dark.

---- ++++ ----

The dwellings are often built of the worst materials, and thus become very speedily out of repair, a state in which they are allowed to remain as long as a tenant can be found for them. The roofs of the rooms I found, in a great number of instances, stained by the water which had percolated through the roofs of the houses; the inhabitants being thus exposed to the injurious effects of damp as well from above, as below.

---- ++++ ----

It is very uncommon for the dwellings to be provided with both front and back yards; where the one is, the other is generally wanting. The immense majority of the back yards are extremely small, and are often greatly encroached upon by a privy.

The dwellings of the poor, in this parish, are, with very few exceptions, destitute of most of those structural conveniences common to the better classes of houses. There are never any places set aside for receiving coals; dust-bins to receive the refuse of the houses are exceedingly rare, and cupboards or closets are nearly altogether unknown. The privies (where there are any attached) are either close to the houses, or at a distance from it, exposed to the public view, or common to large numbers of houses and families. There are never any sinks. The fire-places are constructed without the slightest regard to the convenience or comfort of the inmates"

"Ragged London"

John Hollingshead was a journalist, writer (later a theatre manager!) and came originally from Hoxton so was no stranger to living conditions in the East End.

In 1861 he wrote a book, subtitled "**The Life of London's Poor**" describing living conditions in London, area by area. It is still in print but also available to download as it is out of copyright and worth the effort of reading (search 'THHOL' and the article title)

He mentions his travels through the old Nichol estate. I include some directly relevant sections of his book, but I have amended them slightly for the casual reader to better understand.

> *"That vast district of eastern London familiar to the public under the broad title of Bethnal Green would exhaust a twelvemonth in a house-to-house visitation.*
>
> *It is flat, it is ancient, dirty, and degraded; its courts and alleys are almost countless, and overrunning with men, women, boys, dogs, cats, pigeons, and birds. Its children are ragged, sharp, and weasel-like; brought up from the cradle to hard living and habits of bodily activity.*
>
> *Its men are mainly poor dock labourers, poor costermongers, poorer silk-weavers, clinging hopelessly to a withering handicraft, the lowest kind of thieves, the most ill-disguised class of swell-mobsmen, with a sprinkling of box and toy makers, shoe-makers, and cheap cabinet-makers.*
>
> *Its women are mainly hawkers, seamstresses, the coarsest order of prostitutes, and aged stall-keepers, who often sit at the street corners in old sedan-chairs, and sometimes die, like sentinels, at their posts.*

Its broadest highways are chiefly lined with the most humble shops. There are steaming eating-houses, half filled with puddings as large as sofa squabs, and legs of beef, to boil down into a cheap and popular soup; birdcage vendors; mouldy, musty dens full of second-hand garments, or gay "emporiums" in the ready-made clothing line; pawnbrokers, with narrow, yellow side entrances, whose walls are well marked with the traces of traffic; faded grocers; small print shops, selling periodicals, sweet stuff, and stale fruit; squeezed-up barbers, long factories and breweries, with the black arches of the Eastern Counties Railway running through the midst.

Every street of any pretension is generally guarded at its entrances by public-houses smelling of tobacco, stale beer, and sawdust; and the corners of every leading thoroughfare cutting into the heart of the district are watched over by glittering genii in the shape of gin-palaces.

Concerts, which consist chiefly of street "nigger" singing, held in dingy, long rooms, over the bars of the public-houses in the interior, form the chief amusement of the common inhabitants in their hours of plenty, occasionally varied by dog-fights, rat-matches, and the sport of drawing the badger. On Sundays the whole neighbourhood is like a fair. Dirty men, in their sooty shirt-sleeves, are on the housetops, peeping out of little rough wooden structures built on tile roof to keep their pigeons in. They suck their short pipes, fly their fancy birds, whistle shrilly with their forefingers placed in their mouths, beat the sides of the wooden building with a long stick, like a fishing-rod, and use all their ingenuity to snare their neighbours' stray birds.

Down in some of the streets a regular exchange is held for the purpose of buying, selling, and comparing animals; and, as in Whitechapel and all such neighbourhoods, no difficulty is found in obtaining beer or spirits contrary to law, as long as the money to pay for it is forthcoming.

I have known the neighbourhood I am describing for twenty years, and, if anything, it seems to me to be getting dirtier and more miserable every year. Old houses, in some few places, have been taken away - simply because they fell to pieces; but the new houses erected within the last ten years show little advance in the art of building dwellings for the poor. The whole present plan and arrangement of the district is against improvement, and the new structures sink to the level of the old.

The first court I go into is a square yard - not much larger than a full-sized dining-room. It is entered by a mountainous slope of muddy brick pathway, under an archway; and contains half-a-dozen houses, which look out upon two dust-heaps, a pool of rain and sewage, mixed with rotten vegetable refuse, and a battered, lop-sided public privy.

The houses are like doll's houses, except that they are black and yellow. The windows are everywhere stuffed with paper - rags being in too much demand at the marine store-shop, or for the clothing of the human child-rats, who are digging into the dust-heaps, with muddy oyster-shells. Every child must have its toys; and at the back of Shoreditch they play with rusty old saucepans, pieces of broken china, stones torn out of the roadway, or cinders that they search for laboriously. Very often the boys have to mind babies, while their mothers are out at work, and they sit about upon doorsteps with dirty brown limp bundles that never look like young children.

At the entrance to the square is a row of zigzag two-roomed houses, let for about four shillings a week; the street-doors of which open into the lower rooms, almost upon the wretched tenants' beds. The staircases leading to the upper apartments are little more than ladders in one corner, and there is no space for more than the usual furniture - a table, two chairs, and a bedstead. The flooring of the lower rooms in these houses is so high above the pavement in the street, that three stones are placed at each of the street-doors for the inhabitants to climb into their dwellings by. I say climb, for the lower stone is so lofty, and the whole three are so shallow on their flat surfaces, that it is with difficulty a full-sized man can stride up them. When you stand in the narrow doorway, and look down into the street, it is like looking down into a deep pit. The comfort in the inside of these dwellings is about equal to the conveniences outside. The one we went into smelt so close and musty from overcrowding, neglect, and, perhaps, forty years' dirt, that it almost made me sneeze. It was occupied by a sallow-faced woman, who called herself a "gipsy," and who gets her living amongst servants and others as a fortune-teller.

In another house of greater height, with a close, black, uneven staircase, almost perpendicular, we found a mixed population of about fifty people. In one room was a labourer's wife and several children, yellow, eager, and very ragged; in another was a woman with a blighted eye; in another a girl making match-boxes, assisted by a boy, while her father, a hawker of bootlaces, crouched despondingly over the grate, groaning about the badness of trade, and her mother was busy about the room.

The dirt in this apartment was the landlord's dirt, not the tenant's - a most important distinction. The walls were chipped and greasy - the one cupboard was like a chimney; but the few plates were clean and neatly arranged - clean, perhaps, for want of being used. The floor had been well scrubbed and sanded, the mantelshelf was set out with a few poor china ornaments, and there were a few pictures stuck up which had been cut out of an illustrated newspaper. One was a fancy portrait of Lord Brougham.

This room was admittedly occupied by this family and another woman - a stranger - from necessity, not from choice. At the top of the house was a weaver's work-room, lighted by two long windows with diamond panes. It contained two idle shuttles, watched over by a sickly woman, almost sinking with anxiety, if not from want. The husband was out seeking work in the silk market, like hundreds of fellow-labourers, with little prospect of obtaining it.

A change in fashion, and the inevitable operation of the French Treaty, have affected Spitalfields and Bethnal Green in the same way as Coventry, and a large mass of trained industry finds itself suddenly "displaced." It is not easy in middle life, with energies kept down by low living, little recreation, and bad air, to turn the mind and fingers into a fresh trade. The best of us are not always equal to such a task, and a poor weaver's wife may naturally sit on the edge of her scanty bed, and look into the future with little hope.

The statistics of silk-weaving show a melancholy decline. In 1824 there were 25,000 looms in and about Spitalfields, now there are only 8,000. In 1835 wages were lower by thirty per cent, than in 1824, and they did not average more than eight or nine shillings a week. Now they cannot be higher than seven shillings, or seven shillings and sixpence a week, on an average; and there are only from twenty-five to thirty master weavers. Perhaps, 20,000 working weavers are now struggling against this decay of their handicraft, and many of them, in despair, are taking to street hawking.

I entered another street, not far from the one I have been speaking of, to witness more misery and more pain. There is nothing exceptional or transient in the conditions of life I am endeavouring faintly to describe. In Whitechapel, in St. George's in the East, and in Bethnal Green, the people have lived for nearly a quarter of a century as they are living now. We shall find the social condition of nearly one-half of London to be nearly as low and degraded as that of Ireland in its worst days.

Here is a representative street of houses, the windows in the lower rooms of which are actually on the ground. These lower rooms are wells, dark and unventilated; and overcrowding, with all its attendant evils, can hardly be avoided in such a place. Just now we saw a row of houses where you had to climb up into the lower rooms; here you have to dive down into them.

The first house we enter at random contains a suffering family. A large-headed, gaunt girl, tall and speechless, with arms like thin sticks, sits motionless in a chair. It scarcely requires a second glance at this poor creature to tell that she is an idiot. A man sits shivering by the fire - old-looking though not aged. He is a sawyer by trade. We ask after his health, and his wife, who struggles to speak cheerfully, answers for him:

"He went out, sir, to work, one morning early, without food, and the cold seems to have struck on his chest."

The man tries to tell us that he has never been warm since, but the words seem to hiss in his throat. I have spoken to scores of people who have nearly lost their voices from asthma and other diseases of the chest; and I have seen many poor deaf and dumb creatures who could only show their misery by their looks. One youth - a young coal-whipper, with scanty and uncertain work - was maintaining a father and mother who both suffered under this terrible affliction. The most melancholy sight, however, is to watch the blind when they hear that the visiting clergyman is in the street or court. They creep out of dark holes of doorways, feeling their road carefully, and throw out their arms widely as if to embrace the expected loaf.

A Brief & Incomplete Family History

Christopher Street is a fair sample of an ordinary Bethnal Green street, and though short, it contains many varieties of low and humble life. In one two-roomed house is a notorious dog-trainer, who has lived there for many years, and who keeps a dog-pit for the gratification of his patrons. His yard is often crammed with every kind of terrier and fighting dog, and his upper room, where the pit is built, is reached by a ladder passing through a trap door. When you enter this room, the ladder can be drawn up and the trap-door shut down, and so far you are secure from interruption. The windows are boarded up behind the blinds, so that no noise within can reach the little street; and when a sufficient number of patrons are gathered together to pay the spirited proprietor of this den, the delights of Hockley-in-the-Hole are partially revived. Dogs are set together by the throat, cats are worried and killed by bull-terriers within a certain time, to show the training of the dog, and rats are hunted round the pit for the same purpose.

Within a few doors of this illegal sporting theatre is a family who have just been rescued from the lowest depths of wretchedness. They were found, a few days ago, without food, without fire, or any other necessary, in a room nearly bare, their furniture having been seized for rent. There were a father, mother, and several children standing shivering within the bare walls, the children having nothing on them but sacks tied round their waists.

In Old Nichols Street, a turning in this district leading off from Shoreditch, we have a specimen of an east-end thieves' street. Its road is rotten with mud and water; its houses are black and repulsive; and at least fifty dark sinister faces look at you from behind blinds and dirty curtains as you pass up the rugged pavement.

Courts of the filthiest description branch off on either side, filled with the usual dust-heaps, the usual pools of inky water, and the usual groups of children rolling in the dirt. There is a silence about the street and its houses indicative of the character of the place. The few trades that are carried on are in most cases merely masks - industry is the exception, robbery is the rule. A few hawkers, who have eaten up their "stock money," or capital, and have even pawned their baskets at the baker's for a loaf of bread, are to be found in some of the holes and corners, but the dark public-house with the green blinds is full of thieves, the houses on either side are full of thieves and prostitutes, and a tavern in a side street is full of swell-mobsmen.

Even here, as in all these places, there is something to admire. A woman, who works at box-clump-making, with her husband, has picked an orphan boy from the streets, and given him a place amongst her own children. His father was a porter at one of the markets, and died suddenly in the midst of his work. The boy was tossed about for many days, fighting hard for food, until he found a home with people who were nearly as poor as himself. Many cases of such self-sacrifice, such large-hearted generosity, may be easily found amongst the poor. The cases of heroic endurance under the most frightful trials are even more frequent, and they make us respect these poor creatures even in their dirt and rags.

The Rev. Mr. Trevitt is unceasing in his labours within his own district, and he has called round him an efficient staff of assistants. He has about forty visitors who watch over the poor, and he draws about £80 per annum from the Metropolitan District Visiting Society. He has two ragged schools, which collect about seven hundred children; two national schools, which collect about two hundred and fifty more; and an infant school, which gather about one hundred infants. His Sunday schools are attended by about eight hundred children, who have to work during the week, and his evening schools are generally attended by about eighty of the same class.

There is no public soup-kitchen, but the usual miscellaneous distribution at the parsonage, according to means. Mr. Trevitt looks sharply after the many hungry children in his district, and often has a soup-dinner for these alone. A few days ago a thin, sickly man came to the parsonage door, and asked to be admitted amongst the children. He was told that this was against the rules, and he went away in tears. He was called back before he had crawled out of the street; he crept in, like a poor dog, and was seated with the little ones. His case was inquired into, and it turned out that he was one of the most wretched of that very wretched class, a hospital "incurable." He had been turned out by the doctors a few weeks before, had been tossed about the streets unable to work, and was dying from starvation. His case may be only one out of thousands.

There is a maternity society in the St. Philip's district, to lend necessaries for child-birth, and an excellent industrial school (built and presented to the district by Mr. Edward Thornton, at a cost of £3,000.), where girls and women are taught needlework. The penny bank, in 1860, showed receipts to the amount of £900 and this is the poorest of the Bethnal Green parishes.

The other side of Shoreditch - the Finsbury side - is quite as full of black courts and alleys as Bethnal Green. Walk along the main thoroughfare from the parish church towards the city, peep on one side of the hay-bundle standing at the corn-chandler's door; look through the group of rough, idle loungers, leaning against the corner of the gin-shop, or dive under the fluttering garments that hang across outside the cheap clothier's window, and you will see a dark, damp opening in the wall, like the channel of a sewer passing under and between the houses, and leading to one of the wretched courts and alleys.

You enter the passage, picking your way to the bottom, and find a little square of low, black houses, that look as they were built as a penal settlement for dwarfs. The roofs are depressed, the doors are narrow, the windows are pinched up, and the whole square can almost be touched on each side by a full-grown man. At the further end you will observe a tap, enclosed in a wooden frame, that supplies the water for the whole court, with a dust-bin and privy, which are openly used by all.

In the middle of the little sooty square, standing in the puddles always formed by the sinking stones, you will see three or four harrows belonging to street vendors, and you will gather from this that some of the stall-keepers you have noticed in the thoroughfare outside retire to these dark hiding-places when their labour is done. Glancing over the tattered green curtain at one of the black windows, you will see a room like a gloomy well, and in its depths perhaps a knotted old woman crouching over a small glow-worm of coal, gleaming in a grate full of dust; or the frowning face of some idle male inhabitant of the court, whose expression somehow reminds you of the felon's dock.

If you pass to the right or left, you may find other oven-like entrances leading to other similar courts; or you may go out into the main thoroughfare, and, seeing a similar passage a few yards farther on, you may explore it, to find yourself in another twin huddling-place of the poor. The plan and design of this second court wiil be in all respects the same as those of the first, showing that the same master-mind has created them both. Who the owners of this class of property are may remain a mystery; they draw their rents in short, sharp payments, and they have no reason to complain of the unprofitable character of their investments. These settlements, of which there may be fifty scattered at the backs of the houses on each side of Shoreditch, within the space of half a mile, were all built thirty, forty, sixty, and even eighty years ago, when building regulations were not so strict as they are now; and they were nearly all framed to meet that desire of the English people to have a "house to themselves."

The value of house property in these holes and corners of Shoreditch must be rising rather than falling. An ordinary room, in one of these courts, will fetch two shillings a week, and an ordinary house, which contains little more than one room covered with a loft, will fetch four shillings a week.

In some cases these courts are choked up with every variety of filth; their approaches wind round by the worst kind of slaughter-houses; they lie in the midst of rank stables and offensive trades; they are crowded with pigs, with fowls, and with dogs; they are strewn with oyster-shells and fish refuse; they look upon foul yards and soaking heaps of stale vegetable refuse; their drainage lies in pools wherever it may be thrown; the rooms of their wretched dwellings have not been repaired or whitewashed for years; they are often smothered with smoke, which beats down upon them from some neighbouring factory, whose chimney is beyond the control of the Act of Parliament.

Rag-warehouses have their close store-rooms looking them full in the face; and cats'-meat preparers boil their cauldrons amongst them without fear. In most cases the inhabitants, as we might fully expect, are not superior to their surroundings, and in places like Bowl Court, Plough Yard, which contains a half-Irish colony, they form the greatest nuisance of all. An Irish landlord or landlady will rent a room at about two shillings a week, and then take in as many families, or individuals, at a small nightly rental, as the floor can possibly hold.

This is openly done in defiance of the Lodging-house Act, or any other social reform law.

✻ ✻ ✻

Faces from the 'Old Nichol'

Victorian London was more than just rundown buildings and poor sanitation. Searching through the internet, I came across the following images all taken in or around the Nichol/Shoreditch area between 1850 and 1900.

Stuffing mattresses with straw

Market stall selling Mackerel

A Brief & Incomplete Family History

Clearly, none of the photographs have any direct connection with the POLAIN family, but they show people who lived in the same area of Bethnal Green, at about the same time as our relatives. They allow us to look at the faces and the ordinary lives of people who are long dead, but still, essentially with us.

APPENDIX B

Photographs: A technical note

The earliest photographic images were made in France about 1834 by Louis Daguerre (an artist), closely followed by William Henry Fox Talbot (a chemist) in England. Although Daguerre made his process 'free to the world' this did not apply to England, so early photography was delayed in the UK compared to other countries.

Due to the processes involved, only one original was made and copies were not possible. Coatings were insensitive to light, meaning that the earliest exposures could take up to 60 minutes. Later this would be reduced as the chemistry improved but the immediate consequence was that the first photographs tended to be of buildings rather than people.

The first photographs were (arguably) made with the Daguerreotype process. Invented in 1839 in France, they were almost completely superseded by the newer, less expensive collodion process by 1860.

In the UK, Fox Talbot developed an alternative process but it wasn't until the 1890s when 'tintype' portraits became popular seaside mementoes that photography came to the unwashed masses.

The earliest photographs included in this little family history tend to be very poor quality, in particular of the buildings in the Old Nichol. I suspect this is due to the originals being small or the emulsion deteriorating over time (the chemistry was still hit or miss).

Or we could be looking at scanned copies of copies where the original has been lost. The originals of many photographs taken for reproduction in magazines, periodicals and newspapers have been lost and we only have copies of the 'screened' photograph used by the printers. There is a lot of copying of copies so good quality images take a lot of hunting for. Some may also be in private collections, and therefore not available to the general public.

I am always a little cautious about dates given to photographs when downloaded from the internet. Images have file names and these seldom include a specific date. However, some photographs are so well documented that the dates are known precisely (such as the earliest Fox Talbot images).

Many of the images of the people in the East End are claimed to be from 1850 onwards. However, I suspect that they were taken later (maybe around 1880-1890).

A Brief & Incomplete Family History

There was a huge outcry over the living conditions of the poor in London, and missionaries and campaigners would have paid photographers to take these posed photographs. Many were used for fund raising by the charities.

Technically, they are also better quality photographs with relatively short exposure times, so are unlikely to have been taken using early equipment.

I have included the photographs purely to give a better visual understanding of our ancestors. Study them carefully. Look at the people's clothes, their shoes (and lack of them), the hairstyles.

But most importantly, look at their faces. This is the closest we will ever get to seeing the faces of our ancestors.

APPENDIX C

Weaving: Linen, Silk and Cotton

Types of fabric

From the later middle ages, different textiles were manufactured in a range of weights and could vary greatly in quality. The more finely woven the textile was, the softer and more costly it would be.

Wool
By far the most common fabric (and the core of the flourishing textile industry), wool was knitted or more likely woven. Depending on how it was made, it could be very warm and thick, or light and airy. Wool was also felted for hats and other accessories.

Hemp
Hemp and nettles were used to create workaday fabrics. Though more common for such uses as sails and rope, hemp was also used for clothing.

Linen
Almost as common as wool, linen was made from the flax plant and theoretically available to all classes. Growing flax was labour-intensive and making linen was time-consuming, however. Since the fabric wrinkled easily, it wasn't often found in garments worn by poorer folk. Fine linen was used for the veils and wimples of ladies, undergarments, and a wide variety of apparel and household furnishings.

Cotton
Cotton doesn't grow well in cooler climes, so its use was less common in northern Europe than wool or linen. Still, a cotton industry existed in southern Europe in the 12th century, and cotton became an occasional alternative to linen.

Silk
Luxurious and costly, silk was used only by the wealthiest of classes and the Church.

Dyes
Adding colour was an extra step in the manufacturing process that raised its price, so clothing made from an undyed fabric in various shades of beige and off-white was not uncommon among the poorest folk. A dyed fabric could fade fairly quickly, and bolder shades required either longer dyeing times or more expensive dyes. Thus, the fabrics with the brightest and richest colours cost more and were, therefore, most often found on the nobility and the very rich.

What is Cambric?

Claude Polain and his family were Cambric weavers but what is Cambric?

Cambric was made using flax, which would have been grown locally. It was named after the town of Cambrai in northern France where the techniques were first developed in the 1300s. Today we would call this linen and it is now made with cotton fibres, rather than flax.

Growing flax
The growing cycle is short and sweet, with only 100 days between sowing in March and harvesting in July. The plant ripens by the end of June into golden yellow colour, and then it flowers, dotting the fields with blossoms of violet, blue and white. This display is over quickly, however, for each flax plant blooms for one day only.

Harvesting flax
Flax was harvested by pulling the plant complete with roots, from the ground. It was not cut and harvested like cereal crops. It was then allowed to dry in the field and taken in bundles for 'rippling'.

Rippling was the removal of the seed. Two men at either end of a long board, in the middle of which was fixed a 'rippling comb', did this. The comb looked like a big hairbrush with wooden, or later iron, teeth. It was hard. monotonous work, one man on each side striking alternately.

The flax would then be tied into bundles and taken for soaking in pools of stagnant water. The purpose of this was to let the outer woody part of the flax separate from the inner fibres. This process lasted at least a week.

The flax was dried in the fields and crushed or beaten over a baulk of wood with wooden mallets until the flax stems were completely broken and the bark removed. It was then combed, which drew the fibres out for spinning.

Spinning
Hand-spinning was a cottage industry in pre-industrialization Europe, where the wool spinners (often women and children) would provide enough yarn to service the needs of the men who operated the loom. Claude's wife, together with the other women in the commune, did the spinning and the men did the weaving.

On the eve of the Industrial revolution it took at least five spinners to supply one weaver.

Weaving
The technology of looms was continuously developing so we cant be sure what type of looms were used by Claude. The records refer to them as 'frames' and we can presume that they were treadle operated floor looms. As the 'flying shuttle' wasn't patented until 1733, the looms used by Claude would have had shuttles that were hand thrown, which limited the width of the cloth to the length of a mans arm.

Each of the weavers had four frames, so it would seem that the Apprentices were used to power and operate the looms and the master weavers would supervise.

Bleaching and Dyeing

Finally. after weaving came 'bleaching'. This was the steeping of the cloth in a hot alkaline solution, washing it out, drying the cloth and then applying an acid to neutralise the alkaline. This was repeated until the cloth was as white as required. Bleach fields in and around Dundee and district are well known even today.

Why it matters to us

Cambric was expensive to make and was generally made only for fine shirts, underwear, shirt frills and infant wear.

In the 18th century, after the banning of imports of French fabrics and the availability of cotton from India, the market for Cambric declined. At the same time, there were a number of inventions that changed how fabrics were made.

The cotton gin, used to separate cotton fibres, simplified the process (and reduced the cost). The flying shuttle was invented in 1733 which enabled wider fabrics as well as making weaving faster. The first factories for weaving were built in 1785 and the Jacquard loom was invented about 1803, which enabled the weaving of elaborate patterns using punched cards.

During the early 18th century, cheap cotton was imported from America and powered looms (initially water driven but later steam) became available. In addition, new techniques and dyes enabled the printing of complex patterns on cotton fabrics.

In short, the bottom dropped out of the cambric weaving market, prices for linen collapsed and unemployment of weavers was high. Claude must have been aware of how the world was changing when he moved back from Edinburg to London, but Robert and his children would have been the victims of this economic decline.

The first reliable records of what sorts of jobs people had, and where they lived, are the Census returns, starting in 1841. George, the great grandson of Claude, has his occupation listed as "weaver" in Old Castle Street. His widow, Elizabeth, is listed as a Silk Weaver (hand loom) in 1851. Interestingly, the two other adult residents of the house were also listed as "Silk Weavers" so it is possible that the weaving was carried out in the house (21, Old Nichol Street).

With the decline of linen sales, it appears that Robert or his son George converted from cambric to silk weaving. Cambric was a very fine, high quality fabric, so many of the weaving skills they had would be transferable to silk weaving. In addition, Spitalfields and this part of Bethnal Green had a large and established French Huguenot population and silk weaving was their principal trade.

But the silk trade was also in decline. Wars with France (followed by trade agreements with France) made prices volatile but always high. Silk weaving was labour intensive so as wages increased it became economically unattractive to produce it in England. At the same time the competition from other fabrics increased. High quality printed cotton became available at a low price and soon silk fell out of fashion, even for the very rich.

The independent Silk weavers in the East End found themselves squeezed, with little work, low income and no obvious alternative employment. The competition from the large cotton factories in the north of the country, using large looms and steam power, meant that weaving in London rapidly became a declining trade.

Whilst the silk trade had in the past been very successful, by the 1830s it was already in decline. Although there were 17,000 looms in operation in Spitalfields alone, unemployment was high. In 1860 there was a free trade agreement with France, allowing silks to enter the country at lower cost than those made locally, and the silk trade in England finally collapsed.

Looking at the registers of St. Matthews in Bethnal Green in the late 1700s, about 80% of the church's male parishioners listed their occupation as 'weaver'. It is the female members of the family who tend to list "silk weaving' as an occupation, but this is only seen after the census started in 1840. Occupations for the men such as plasterer, painter, printer and shoe/boot maker become progressively more frequent in the census returns of our ancestors.

APPENDIX D

The French Hospital

A number of the family depended on the French Hospital in the later part of their lives. The Hospital was seen as a safe refuge for people who couldn't support themselves, and the applicants had to demonstrate their Huguenot credentials to be accepted.

The records of the Hospital (in French) still exist but are not readily available. If time permits it would be interesting to examine them for more insights into the lives of our ancestors.

The Pest House

The original 'French hospital 'was the Pest House in the fields where Bath Street is now situated. Built in 1594 it served to isolate those suffering from such incurable or infectious diseases as leprosy and the plague from the City of London.

From 1693 to 1718 the Pest House was used for sick French Protestant refugees until the French Hospital was built on an adjacent site.

The French Hospital

The first French Protestant Hospital was established in 1718 in Bath Street, off City Road, as an almshouse for the relief of poor or distressed Huguenots. The Hospital was greatly supported by the wealthier Huguenots, who were proud that none of their people would be forced to beg. Members of the community took care of those who were poor, elderly, frail, mentally disturbed or chronically ill.

The Hospital was initiated by the gift of £1,000 towards the founding of such an institution by Jacques de Gastigny, who had died in 1708. The money was invested and, as successive benefactions were added, the fund grew.

In 1716 a plot of land in a bye-lane (now Bath Street) off Old Street was purchased. Some adjoining land was leased from the City of London to form a site of some 4 acres on which to build the almshouse.

The French Hospital about 1750

The Hospital opened in November 1718 with 80 beds. Over the years more buildings were added to the site. By 1760 some 234 inmates were accommodated at what was affectionately known as La Providence.

However, by the middle of the 19th century, the buildings had become greatly dilapidated and were in urgent need of repair. The Directors of the Hospital decided it would be simpler to rebuild the institution somewhere else. A new site was sought and, in 1862, three acres of land in South Hackney were purchased for £3,600.

The (new) French Hospital about 1870

The new French Protestant Hospital opened in June 1865. Built in a kind of Gothic style, it resembled a small French chateau. It had accommodation for 40 women and 20 men, and was staffed by a Steward and his wife, together with nurses and servants. As well as spacious Day Rooms, there was a Library and a chapel. Inmates were encouraged not to be idle but to make themselves useful by helping towards the running of the institution.

In 1887, to mark her Jubilee, Queen Victoria was presented with a black silk dress made by 12 female inmates of the Hospital, all weavers.

In 1934 the Hospital was threatened with a compulsory purchase order by the LCC, but WW2 intervened. In 1941 the inmates were evacuated and the building requisitioned. It then became a Day Nursery for mothers working for the war effort.

Present day

The South Hackney building was taken over by St Victoire's Convent School in 1949. In 1973 it became an annexe for the Lower School of the Cardinal Pole Catholic School (the Upper School was in Kenworthy Road). The building is still there and can easily be seen from the main road.

The original Hospital buildings in Bath Street (off Old Street) have been demolished. Their site is now occupied by St Luke's C of E Primary School.

APPENDIX E

What was (is) a Calvanist?

Claude Polain escaped to England in 1724 due to the persecution of non Catholics in France. The background to this is explained in Chapter 1.

Words Huguenot, Protestant and Calvinist are used interchangeably although they were different things.

Who was Calvin?

John Calvin (1509-1564) was a French priest who was a key figure in the **Protestant Reformation**. Born in Picardy, by the age of 12 he was employed as a clerk by the Bishop and later went to university in Paris (and later to Orleans) to study Latin, Greek and the law.

At some stage he became a priest but became increasingly unhappy in the Catholic church. In this he wasn't alone as there were a number of radical thinkers in Europe at that point who suggested the church needed to be reformed. In fact, Martin Luther (1483-1546), a monk in Wittenberg (Germany) had published his concerns about the church as early as 1517 and unwittingly gave birth to Protestant Reform.

He finally broke from the Roman Catholic Church around 1536 when he published his thoughts in "Institutes of the Christian Religion". Numerous texts followed and eventually Calvin ended up in Strasbourg and Geneva.

Over the years Calvin's views on the church hardened and grew wider, and after his death his views became the basis of 'Calvinism' within Protestantism. The label 'Calvinism' can be misleading, because the religious tradition it denotes has always been diverse, with a wide range of influences rather than a single founder. There is a huge number of 'reformed' churches, and Presbyterian (Scotland), Congregationalist (USA) and Baptist churches all have their origins in Calvin's 'reformed' church.

Unlike Calvinism, Lutheranism retains many of the practices of the pre-Reformation Catholic Church. Lutheranism was confined to Germany and Scandinavia, but Calvinism spread to England, France, the Netherlands and to North America.

What does a Calvinist believe?

Calvinism shares some of the same beliefs as other branches of the Reformation. It emphasises the sovereignty of God and the authority of the Bible:

- The Bible is the only basis for faith and life including a literal interpretation of the book of Genesis;

- The Pope has no authority;
- All human beings would be eternally damned were it not for divine intervention;
- God has chosen some human beings for eternal salvation in heaven (**predestination**!);
- Calling your children after Catholic saints was forbidden;
- God calls individuals to salvation, they cannot refuse even if they want to;
- Once people have been saved by God, those people cannot lose their salvation through any act of their own;

In the 17th Century, Calvanists would have been expected to attend church regularly, would have encouraged simplicity in dress and forbidden many forms of enjoyment such as drinking alcohol, dancing, singing and playing cards. Of course, there would be a wide range of compliance among the congregation, so younger members of the church would no doubt have been less rigorous in their adherence.

Who are Calvanists?

All Calvinist are Protestants, not all Protestants are Calvinist.

i) The word "**Protestant**" broadly means any Christian who is not a Catholic or Orthodox;

ii) "**Huguenot**" refers to a follower of the French Reform Church, which has Calvinist roots. More generally it was used to describe a Protestant seeking sanctuary from the Catholic Church and its Catholic followers;

iii) "**Church of England**" or "**Anglicans**". Originally a catholic church not recognising the authority of the Pope but instead under the control of the King or Queen of England.

iv) "**Puritans**" were a strict Protestant group that existed mostly in England in the 17th Century. Due to their views they came into conflict with the authorities and many sought refuge in America (i.e. Pilgrim Fathers etc.). Over time, laws and attitudes in England changed and Puritanism declined in the 18th Century.

APPENDIX F

East London Churches

A Tale of Three Churches

The first obvious question is, why should we be interested in the Churches in East London? However, three Churches in particular played an important role in documenting the POLAIN family for nearly 200 years.

*When Claude came to London, he registered at The **French Protestant Church** in Threadneedle Street, which was a centre for the Calvinist French community. This church is long gone but has provided the documentary evidence for Claude's life.*

*When the family moved to Bethnal Green, they registered at **St. Matthews** Church. Although rebuilt and repaired over the years, a similar looking church still sits on the same plot of land.*

*As the family expanded, some of them had births, deaths or marriages recorded at **St. Leonards** in Shoreditch. The church today remains relatively unchanged after 300 years.*

It is due to the French Church, St. Matthews and St. Leonards that we have such a good record of the POLAIN family. In addition, as both St. Matthew and St. Leonard churches still exist, they provide excellent markers on the ground. All the maps I have included (see **Appendix H**) have the churches ringed so the reader has some understanding of scale and distance.

French Churches

French Protestant Churches were established by refugees from persecution in France, which was particularly heavy following the Revocation of the Edict of Nantes in 1685. They settled in two main areas of London, Spitalfields and Soho,

The French Church was founded on July 24, 1550 when Edward VI gave a charter to Protestant refugees led by a Polish minister, Jean a Lasco. By the charter of 1550, the names of new pastors were to be submitted to the sovereign for approbation. This is still observed today.

The French Protestant Church in Threadneedle Street, London between 1669 and 1841. Many Huguenots who came to London registered at the church

The charter granted to the refugees the right to worship according to their own manner and to establish a church at Austin Friars in the city of London. As some of the refugees spoke Dutch and others spoke French, the two congregations soon separated.

The French Huguenots took a lease of land in Threadneedle Street which they were to occupy from 1550 to 1841 (except during the reign of Mary Tudor). A strict and continental Calvinist form of worship was practiced.

The "L'Eglise Protestant" was originally based in a medieval chapel in Thread Needle Street but was destroyed in the Great Fire of London in 1666. The building was rebuilt by the congregation in 1669 and could accommodate 1000 people. Following the Revocation of the Edict of Nantes by Louis XIV of France in 1685, many other French churches were founded in London, but not one of these has survived to the present time. The construction of new churches and the organization of financial aid and charities (hospital, schools, and soup kitchens) made it possible to cope with the influx of Huguenots to the area.

By 1700 there were nine French churches in the East End (all of which practiced a Calvinist form of worship), and twelve in the West End (six of which celebrated Anglican communion, and six a Calvinist liturgy).

The Threadneedle Street church set up its own charity in 1718 for poor relief, the French Hospital "La Providence" in Clerkenwell (**see Appendix D**).

The French Protestant Church was demolished in 1841 to make way for the new Royal Exchange building. There had been two previous Royal Exchanges, both destroyed by fire.

By this stage the majority of French Protestants in London were in the Soho area so the congregation at Threadneedle Street had declined.

However, the location of the Church is still clearly shown in the 1896 Ordnance Survey map, but the site was now occupied by a Bank. The current building is different to the buildings on either side so it is easy to identify the original plot occupied by the Church.

A new church was established in St. Martine-Le-Grand where it remained until 1887, when it was demolished to make way for extensions to the adjoining General Post Office. The congregation then moved into temporary quarters at the Athenaeum Hall, Tottenham Court Road, until a suitable site for another church could be purchased and a new building erected.

After two years of enquiry it was decided to purchase a plot of land in Soho Square. The existing buildings at this site were to be demolished to provide a combined frontage to the square of fifty feet and a depth of one hundred and ten feet. The freehold was owned by a Mr. Trotter, who sold the site for £10,500. Building work cost another £10,000.

Whilst the "L'Eglise Protestant" is long gone, the site of it is easy to find by just following the maps through the ages. The site of the Church is still clearly shown in the 1896 Ordnance Survey map but was now occupied by a Bank. The current building is different to the buildings on either side so it is easy to identify the original plot occupied by the Church.

Appendix H shows the location of the church and how the area around it has changed over the years.

Other French Protestant Churches in East London

    Church of the Artillery (French Church), Artillery Lane

    Eglise Neuve (French Church), Church Street

    French Church, Crispin Street

    French Church, Pearl Street

    French Church, Wheeler Street

    Independent Chapel, Hope St

    La Patente de Spitalfields or La Nouvelle Patente, Paternoster Row /Brown's Lane

    Répertoire Générale (Huguenot community general register),

    St. Jean (French Church), John Street

    French Church, Swan Fields, Shoreditch

Spitalfields Churches

Spitalfields: the fields to the east of medieval priory and hospital of St. Mary Spital. A mainly rural area up to the beginning of the 17th century but by 1640 there had been some building along the southern and eastern fringes spreading from Whitechapel and the City. Rapid development in the next three decades brought the number of houses to about 1300, mostly small tenements crowded into narrow streets and alleyways.

Many foreigners, including French weavers, were already present by the time of the large influx of Huguenot refugees from France after the Revocation of the Edict of Nantes in 1685. Spitalfields gained the reputation in the 18th century as the centre of production of fine silks and in 1807 the population had reached over 15,000.

The slum buildings were being replaced by blocks of artisans' dwellings beginning with the first Peabody Buildings in Commercial Street in 1864. The new buildings were mainly occupied by Jewish immigrants who came into the area in increasing numbers from the 1880's, the weaving trade being replaced by small furriers' and clothing workshops.

One building at the corner of Fournier Street and Brick Lane reflects the social changes that have occurred in Spitalfields. Built as a Huguenot chapel in 1743, it later became a Wesleyan chapel, a synagogue and is now a mosque.

Christ Church, Commercial St

Christ Church Spitalfields was erected in 1714-1729 to cater for the rapidly growing population and as an attempt to combat the nonconformity of the area that had existed from 1612 with the first Baptist church in England.

Stepney Churches

The Domesday Book of 1086 describes Stepney as an arable area with meadows, pastures and woodland with a population of 900 which included Hackney. In medieval times the parish of Stepney extended east from the City as far as the River Lea and north from the River Thames as far as Hackney.

At the end of the 16th century there was a period of rapid growth in population with the development of the riverside and eastern suburbs of the City. For civil purposes Stepney had been divided up into four hamlets - Ratcliffe, Limehouse, Poplar and Mile End, but because of the increase in buildings and inhabitants new hamlets were created. Bethnal Green (in 1597), Shadwell (in 1645), Spitalfields (in 1662), St. George in the East (in 1670), Mile End New Town (in 1691) and Bow (in 1719). Whitechapel and Bromley St. Leonard were already separate parishes.

The name Stepney now meant little more than a geographical area around St. Dunstan's church but revived in the 19th century as the name of a registration district.

During World War Two more than a third of the houses were made uninhabitable and most of the others damaged by bombing, as were the docks, warehouses and business premises. Stepney became part of the London Borough of Tower Hamlets in 1965.

St. Dunstan and All Saints, Stepney High St.

St Dunstan and All Saints Church, in Stepney High Street, is a church of great antiquity. About the year 952 Dunstan, Bishop of London and Lord of the Manor of Stepney, replaced the small wooden church on this site with a new stone church dedicated to All the Saints.

When Dunstan was canonised in 1029 the name was changed to St Dunstan and All Saints.

Until the early 1300s, when new churches were built at Whitechapel and Bow, this church served the whole of Middlesex east of the City of London - an enormous area.

The present church is the third one on this site and dates mainly from the 1400s although the chancel, where the altar stands, is 200 years older. The church has been much repaired outside including porches and an octagonal parish room added in 1872.

There have been a number of interior renovations over the years and the latest ones have cleared out many of the earlier additions to show the original architecture to its best advantage.

A Brief & Incomplete Family History

The bells are commemorated in the rhyme 'Oranges and Lemons'...."When will that be, say the bells of Stepney". The oldest of the ten bells was recast in 1385.

The churchyard was once famous for its crowded mass of tombstones, of which only a few 18th century table tombs remain. In the 1600s the churchyard was enlarged to make room for victims of the plague - no less than 6,583 within an 18-month period and 154 on one day alone. As you can tell, there is not much chance of finding an ancestor's grave here but the grounds are pleasant and park-like if you need a rest after too much walking.

Other Churches in Stepney

Christ Church, Jamaica St
East London Mission to the Jews, Commercial Rd
St. Anthony, Globe Rd
St. Augustine, Settle St
St. Faith, Shandy St
St. John, Halley St, Limehouse Fields
St. Luke, Burdett Rd
St. Mark, Goodman's Fields
St. Matthew, Salmon Lane
St. Paul, Bow Common
St. Paul, Dock St
St. Philip, Newark St
St. Saviour and the Cross, Wellclose Sq
St. Thomas, Arbour Sq.
Baptist Chapel, James St
Congregational Chapel, Cannon Street Rd
Congregational Chapel, Burdett Rd
Globe Fields Burial Ground (Wesleyan Methodist)
Independent Chapel,
Independent Meeting House, Bull Lane
Independent Meeting House, New Road
Latimer Chapel, formerly Mile End Road Chapel, Bridge St

Bethnal Green Churches

Bethnal Green is situated about 1½ miles north of Whitechapel and ¾ mile northeast of Shoreditch and was originally part of the Manor of Stepney.

It was the poorest district of Victorian London but two hundred years earlier was a pleasant country area with wealthy residents. By the end of the 17th century the silk-weavers of Spitalfields began spreading into the area and by the mid 18th century it was said to have eighteen hundred houses with fifteen thousand inhabitants - three or four families in a house.

By 1840 there were six times as many looms used in Bethnal Green than in Spitalfields and Mile End New Town. Although the weaving industry was in decline, other industries based at home or in small workshops took its place.

St. Matthew, St. Matthew's Row

St Matthew's was formed from part of the parish of St Dunstan and All Saints, Stepney, in 1746, due to the increase in population. Building commenced in 1743 and was completed by 1746 to a design by George Dance the Elder.

The drawing is St Matthews in 1818. The church we see nowadays was rebuilt in 1859 after a fire; and re-built again after severe damage in the Second World War (see photo).

St. Mathews in 1818

From 1837 onwards, St Matthew's parish was itself divided into a number of smaller parishes and the Bethnal Green Registration District ended up with 17 churches in its area, the majority of which were built between 1840 and 1845.

With the burgeoning of scientific discovery in 18th century England, it became necessary to protect the buried corpses in the churchyard from desecration by "resurrectionists"

St. Mathews as it is today

Medical schools at Guy's and the new London Hospitals were not overly-fussy where the bodies for their research and teaching actually came from. In 1754 the Watch House was built and by 1792 a person was paid 10s 6d per week to be on guard. A reward of 2 guineas was granted for the apprehension of any body snatchers and the watchmen were provided with a blunderbuss and permission to fire it but only after sounding a rattle.

The graveyard quickly filled up and burials halted. The church graveyards in Bethnal Green were so full, they were considered a health risk and there were numerous complaints about the smell. By 1850 public cemeteries had taken the place of the church graveyard.

When the church was damaged by bombing during the war, the graveyard was so severely damaged that only two headstones remained undamaged. When the church was re-built after the war, the graveyard was cleared and replaced by open parkland.

St. James the Great, Bethnal Green Rd

St James the Great was completed in 1844 and was formed from part of the parish of St Matthew's, Bethnal Green. During the 1990s it was deconsecrated and has since been remodelled into flats (apartments).

It is situated on the busy Bethnal Green Road and has no surrounding churchyard or garden - it's right out there on a street corner! It was in the Bethnal Green Registration District and, in 1965, became part of the London Borough of Tower Hamlets.

St. James the Great, Bethnal Green

St John on Bethnal Green was built in 1826-1828 to a design by Sir John Sloane and was extensively repaired in 1871 after a fire. It was formed from part of the parish of St Matthew's, Bethnal Green when the area grew in population.

It is situated on one corner of the major crossroads at Bethnal Green Road and Roman Road and Cambridge Heath Road. It was in the Bethnal Green Registration District and, in 1965, became part of the London Borough of Tower Hamlets.

St John on Bethnal Green

A Brief & Incomplete Family History

St. Jude, Old Bethnal Green Rd. was demolished during post war redevelopment of the bomb damaged area. The site now open ground between residential apartment buildings. A small turning off Old Bethnal Green Road at the old location of the Church is now called St. Jude's Road.

St. Jude, Old Bethnal Green Rd

Other Churches in Bethnal Green

St. Peter, St. Peter's Ave
Holy Trinity, Old Nichol St
Jew's Episcopal Chapel
St. Andrew, Viaduct St
St. Barnabas, Grove Rd
St. Bartholomew, Coventry Rd
St. Philip, Swanfield St
St. Matthias, Cheshire St
St. Paul, Virginia Rd
St. Simon Zelotes, Morpeth St
St. Thomas, Baroness Rd
Domestic Mission Chapel (Presbyterian), Spicer St / Mansford St
Gibraltar Burial Ground (Dissenters)
Independent Chapel, Cambridge Rd
Independent Chapel, Sydney St
United Reformed Church (previously Congregational)

Shoreditch Churches

Shoreditch is situated about a mile north of Whitechapel. The original settlement was founded at the junction of two Roman Roads, Kingsland Road and Old Street. St. Leonard's church was founded about the 12th century, the parish also including Hoxton and Haggerston. The land in the parish was owned by Holywell Priory, the hospital of St. Mary Spital, the Canons of St. Paul and the Bishop of London.

St. Leonard, Shoreditch High St.

St Leonard's Church, in Shoreditch High Street, was probably founded in the 12th century and includes in its parish the hamlets of Hoxton and Haggerston, both of which are mentioned in the Domesday Book.

It is the ancient church of the original parish and all the subsequent, smaller parishes in the Shoreditch RD were created from this one, mainly in the mid-1800s when the population was growing rapidly.

Part of the tower gave way during a service in 1716 and the church was rebuilt by George Dance in 1736-1740.

St. Leonard in 1740

The spire is an imitation of Wren's magnificent steeple on St Mary-le-Bow in Cheapside. The whipping post and village stocks are still in the churchyard.

The interior has sombre woodwork, a flat panelled ceiling and there were galleries on both sides of the nave which were removed in 1857. The church was damaged in the 2nd World War but has since been repaired.

The bells are commemorated in the rhyme 'Oranges and Lemons'...."When I grow rich, say the bells of Shoreditch".

St. Leonard as it is today

Other Churches in Shoreditch
All Saints, Haggerston Rd
St. Agatha, Finsbury Ave
St. Anne, Hoxton St
St. Augustine, Yorkton St
St. James, Curtain Rd
St. Mark, Old St
St. Michael, Mark St
St. Peter, Hoxton Square
Acadamy Chapel, Hoxton St
Baptist Chapel, Worship St
Calvinist Methodist Chapel, Cumberland St / Curtain Rd
Ebenezer Chapel (Bible Christian), Old Street Rd
Geffery's Almshouses Chapel, Kingsland Rd
Holywell Mount Chapel (Congregational), Chapel St / Curtain Rd
Methodist Chapel formerly Middlesex Chapel, Hackney Rd
Shoreditch Workhouse, Kingsland Rd

APPENDIX G

Unidentified Persons

I went through all the **UK Indexes** for the **Births, Marriages and Deaths** between 1840 and 1910, expecting this to confirm what I already knew of the family.

What I wasn't expecting was to find a significant number of names that I could not place.

For births, this could be partly explained by the high child mortality rate, but you would still expect the unknown Births and (matching name) Deaths to pretty much cancel things out.

I was wrong.

The information associated with the Death Certificates is unreliable. People register the death using the dead persons preferred name (i.e. Joseph was listed as Joe; Elizabeth was listed as Eliza, Liza, Liz or any one of half a dozen variants) instead of their baptised names, and dates of births are often estimates.

I have even found a case where a women was christened with one name but was listed on the census with a slightly different name. She even signed her wedding certificate with her assumed name, despite the fact that the Vicar had written her original name on it. I don't suppose she even had any idea she had been christened with a different name.

Marriage Certificates where you have no other records that match (Birth or Death) also cause problems, and unless you have access to the parish records, you can't narrow it down using Father's name, addresses or the names of witnesses.

The aim now is to go back through the birth records and to see if we can identify the current unknowns. This is unlikely to be a quick or easy exercise.

Births

Male births that I haven't connected to the family tree.

Surname	Christian Names	Gender	Date	Qtr.
Polain	Albert Edward	Male	1861	1
Polain	Claud	Male	1868	2
Polain	Claud Albert	Male	1894	3
Polain	Edmund Sidney T	Male	1896	3
Polain	George John	Male	1893	3
Polain	George John	Male	1902	3
Polain	Henry	Male	1854	4
Polain	Herbert George	Male	1896	4
Polain	Herbert John	Male	1873	3
Polain	James	Male	1868	3

Polain	John Joseph	Male	1899	2
Polain	William	Male	1851	2
Polain	William	Male	1849	2
Polain	William George	Male	1890	3
Polain	William James	Male	1865	3
Polaine	Albert Edward	Male	1886	3
Polaine	Alfred William	Male	1901	3
Polaine	Charles	Male	1899	1
Polaine	Charles James L	Male	1904	1
Polaine	Daniel Thomas	Male	1909	
Polaine	Leslie Francis	Male	1905	3
Polaine	Thomas W.P.	Male	1904	3
Polaine	William	Male	1880	3

Marriages

Male marriages that I haven't connected to the family tree.

Surname	Christian Names	Gender	Date	Qtr.
Polain	John J.	Male	1866	4
Polain	William	Male	1854	1
Polaine	Claude	Male	1889	4
Polaine	Daniel Thomas	Male	1908	
Polaine	Daniel T	Male	1939	
Polaine	James Leonard	Male	1881	2
Polaine	Peter	Male	1883	3
Polaine	Peter	Malc	1910	
Polaine	Peter	Male	1916	
Polaine	William	Male	1876	3

Deaths

Male deaths that I haven't connected to the family tree.

Surname	Christian Names	Gender	Date	Qtr.
Polain	Albert Edward	Male	1862	3
Polain	George Peter	Male	1849	3
Polain	Henry	Male	1864	2
Polain	James	Male	1870	4
Polain	John	Male	1844	3
Polain	John	Male	1849	1
Polain	William	Male	1849	4
Polain	William	Male	1852	3
Polain	William	Male	1864	1
Polain	William	Male	1881	2

Polaine	Claude Albert	Male	1898	2
Polaine	Daniel	Male	1867	1
Polaine	Herbert George	Male	1900	1
Polaine	Peter	Male	1904	1
Polaine	Robert John	Male	1904	4

APPENDIX H

Maps & Diagrams

Polain Family Homes and their Surroundings	147
Edinburgh, Scotland (Maps A1 to A5)	151
Bethnal Green, London (Maps B1 to B9)	156
Threadneedle Street (Bank), London (Maps C1 to C5)	165
Sample Census Forms	170
Simplified Descendents Chart (inside cover)	

Polain Family Homes and their Surroundings

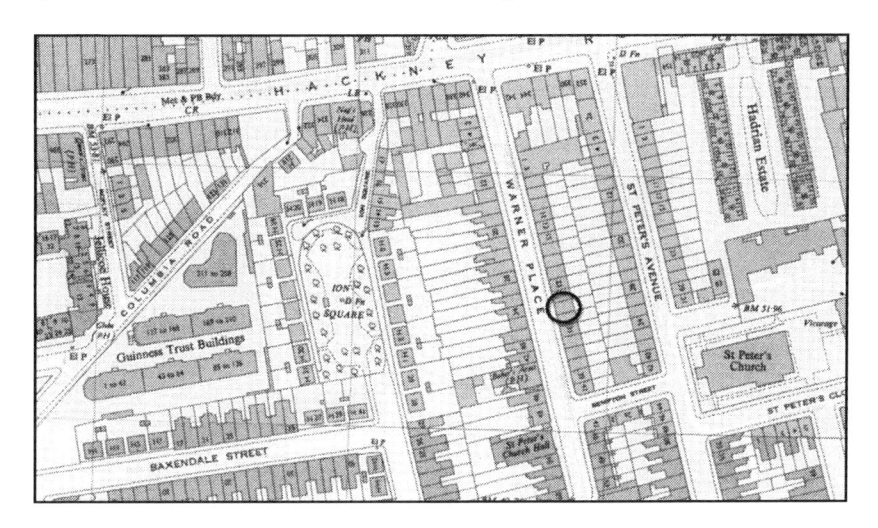

John Albert POLAIN lived at **27 Warner Place** (1881 Census). It is not known how long the family lived at this address but other family members lived in Warner Place around the same time.

Despite the attentions of the Luftwaffe, Warner Place and the surrounding streets survived the war intact. It was the Town Planners in the years following the war that destroyed 'old' Bethnal Green. The street map below shows the area now.

Apart from Baxendale Street (which remains unchanged) I can only find two buildings in the area which have survived from the 1890s. The most obvious is St. Peter's Church but in Warner Place there is a small building (which may have been a chapel or church hall) which has survived and would have been recognisable to John Albert.

The picture is of a surviving house of the same period in Baxendale Street. The area has become quite desirable as it is within easy walking and cycling distance of the City.

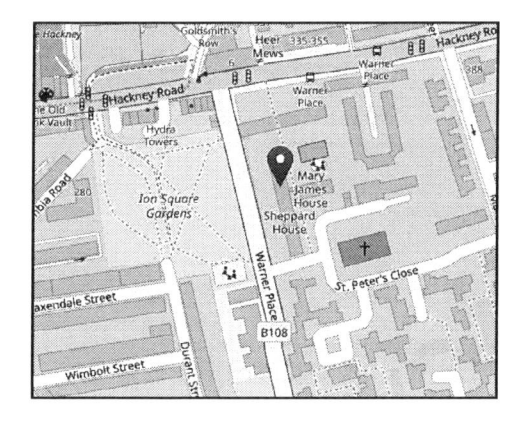

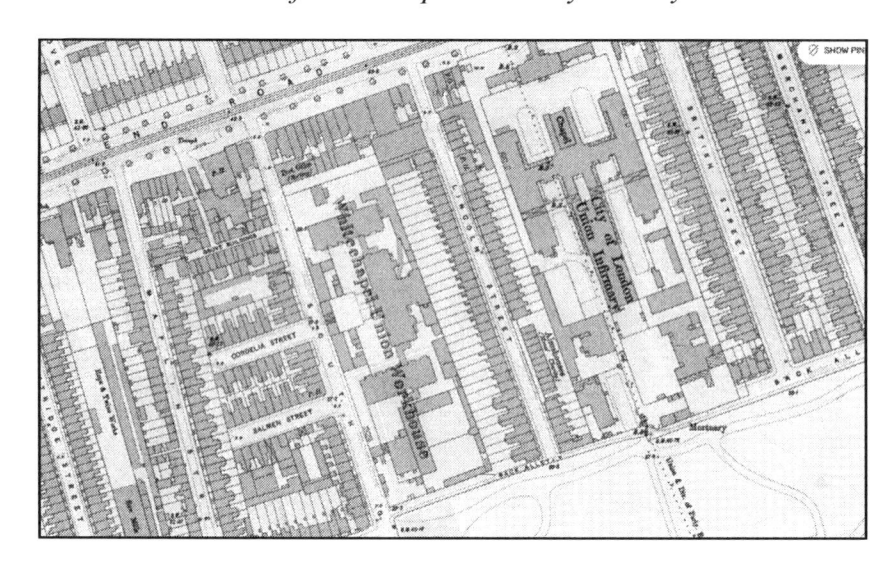

By the time of the 1901 Census, John and Jane were living in **Lincoln Street,** a turning off Mile End. The house they lived in backed onto the Infirmary and is now gone-possibly as a result of a fire at the Infirmary in 1935.

The picture to the left is a house across the street, which is the same as the one where John and Jane lived.

The area is interesting for a number of reasons. In the 1830s looking after the poor of a parish was not a State responsibility but a local one. The Poor Commissioners grouped 108 London Parishes together to form the **City of London Union** and the **East London Union**. These Unions operated workhouses on behalf of the Parishes.

The City of London Union was a wealthy Union but did not have their own workhouse. After years of complaints (paupers were farmed out to Contractors outside London), in 1849 a workhouse was built. It was designed to take 800 inmates and included central heating and a private chapel. However, the new workhouse had room only for those casual applicants deemed sick and helpless-healthy ones would be refused admittance.

By 1869, the Union had enlarged and the **Bow Workhouse** officially became the **City of London Union's Infirmary**. In 1936 the Infirmary was renamed **St. Clement's Hospital** and became part of the NHS but in recent years it has been converted into blocks of luxury flats.

The **Whitechapel Union Workhouse** was built in 1871 to the west of Lincoln Street but was known to many as the South Grove workhouse as that is where the main entrance was (now Southern Grove). The buildings could accommodate 800 inmates.

By the 1930s the building had been taken over by the LCC and was used for a variety of purposes including a day centre before falling into disuse.

The site is now part of a Tower Hamlets conservation area and the building on the right in the photograph is being preserved, although surrounded by blocks of flats. It is not clear what the building will be used for in future.

To the south of Lincoln Street is the **City of London and Tower Hamlets Cemetery.** Opened in 1841 and closed to burials in 1966 there are over 350,000 people buried here.

Before the Victorian era, all of London's dead were buried in small urban churchyards, which were so overcrowded and so close to where people lived, worked, and worshipped that they were causing disease and ground water contamination.

An Act of Parliament was passed which allowed private companies to purchase land and set up large cemeteries outside the boundaries of the City of London. There were seven great cemeteries laid out about the same time (1832–41) including Highgate and Abney Park.

Tower Hamlets Cemetery was very popular with people from the East End and by 1889 247,000 bodies had been interred, most in public graves. Public graves were the property of the company and were used to bury those whose families could not afford to buy a plot.

Several persons, entirely unrelated to each other, could be buried in the same grave within the space of a few weeks.

The cemetery itself did not remain in a tidy and elegant state for long. By 1986 Tower Hamlets had taken it over and by 2000 declared it a Nature Reserve. The cemetery now resembles natural woodland, with many bird and insect species making it their home, although there are still a large amount of gravestones and funerary monuments.

John Albert and Jane moved out of the East End to 35 Arkley Road, Walthamstow before 1911 (see census return-in 1911, John and Jane had 5 children). However, they had moved to **42, Haroldstone Road** by 1912 for the birth of their son William Arthur.

Walthamstow was an attractive option for people from Bethnal Green and the surrounding area. It had parks and open spaces, schools nearby and affordable (and modern) housing. But it was the opening of the Liverpool Street to Chingford rail line that was the big draw. For only a few pence, the East Enders could easily and cheaply commute to their existing jobs in the East End.

The scale of movement from the East End to Walthamstow was significant. Charles Booth, a social reformer, described the area to the south of St. James Street (between the railway and the River Lea) as "Little Bethnal Green".

Three generations of POLAINs lived at no. 42 before they moved further afield.

Edinburgh, Scotland

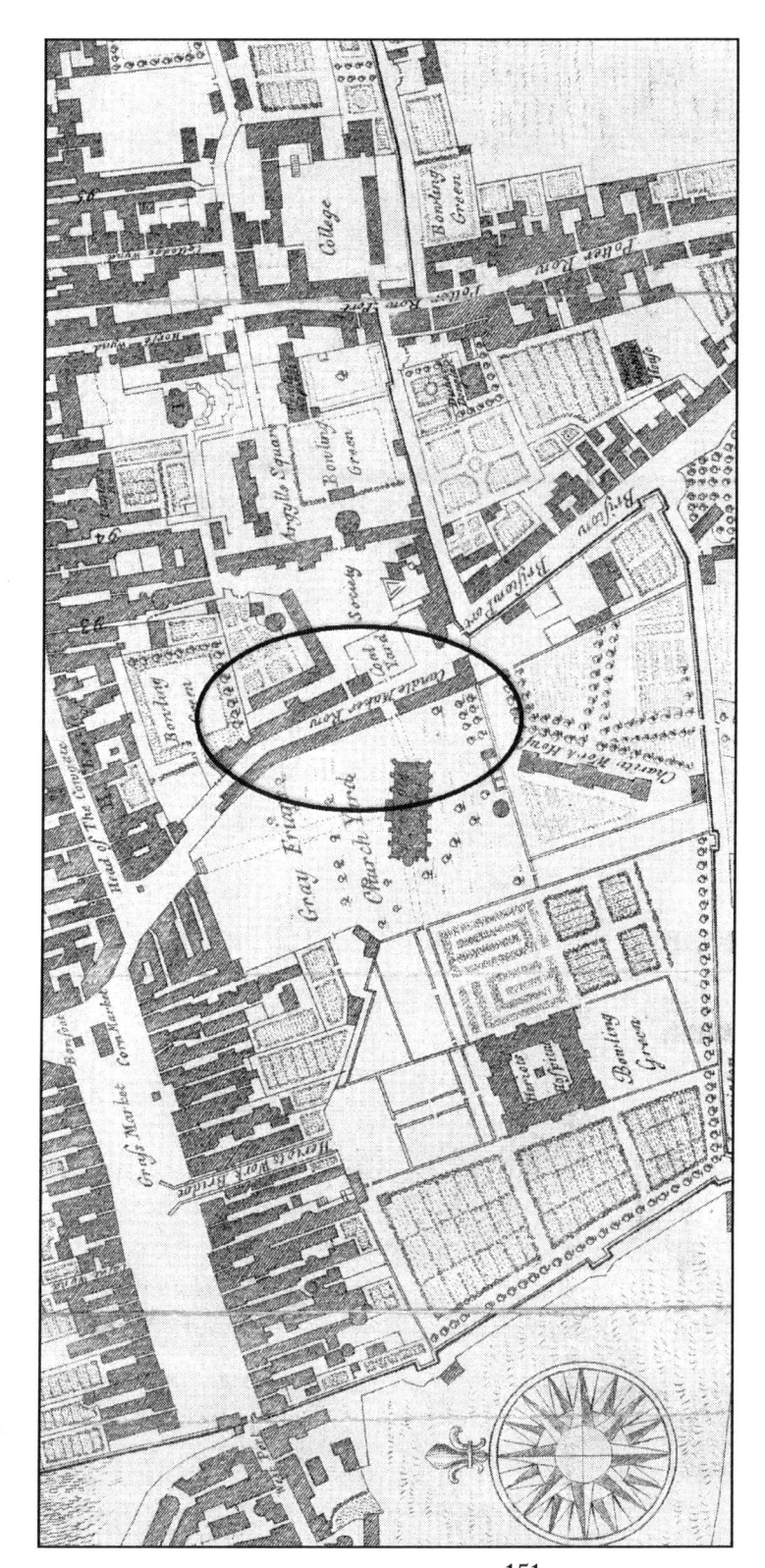

MAP A1 – 1742 (Daniel Lizars). When Claude and the other Cambric weavers first moved to Edinburgh they stayed at accommodation in Candle Maker Row. Judging by its proximity to the Church and the Bowling Greens it was probably one of the better areas of the city to stay in (if we ignore the nearby Coal Yard and Work House).

A Brief & Incomplete Family History

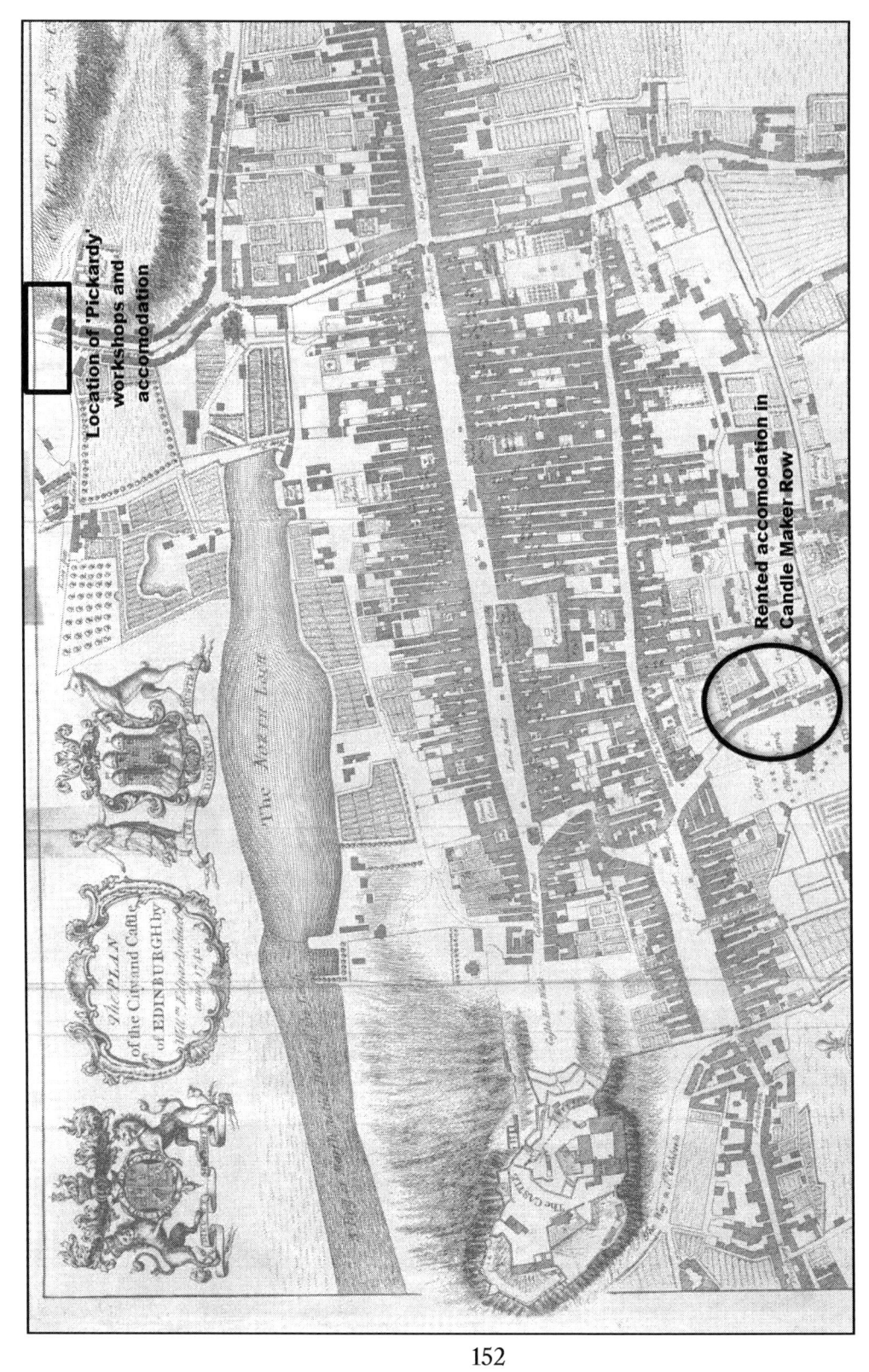

MAP A2 – 1742 (Daniel Lizars). New workshops were constructed for the weavers. This map of the town shows the location of their temporary accommodation and the location of the workshops near Calton Hill (just outside map).

A Brief & Incomplete Family History

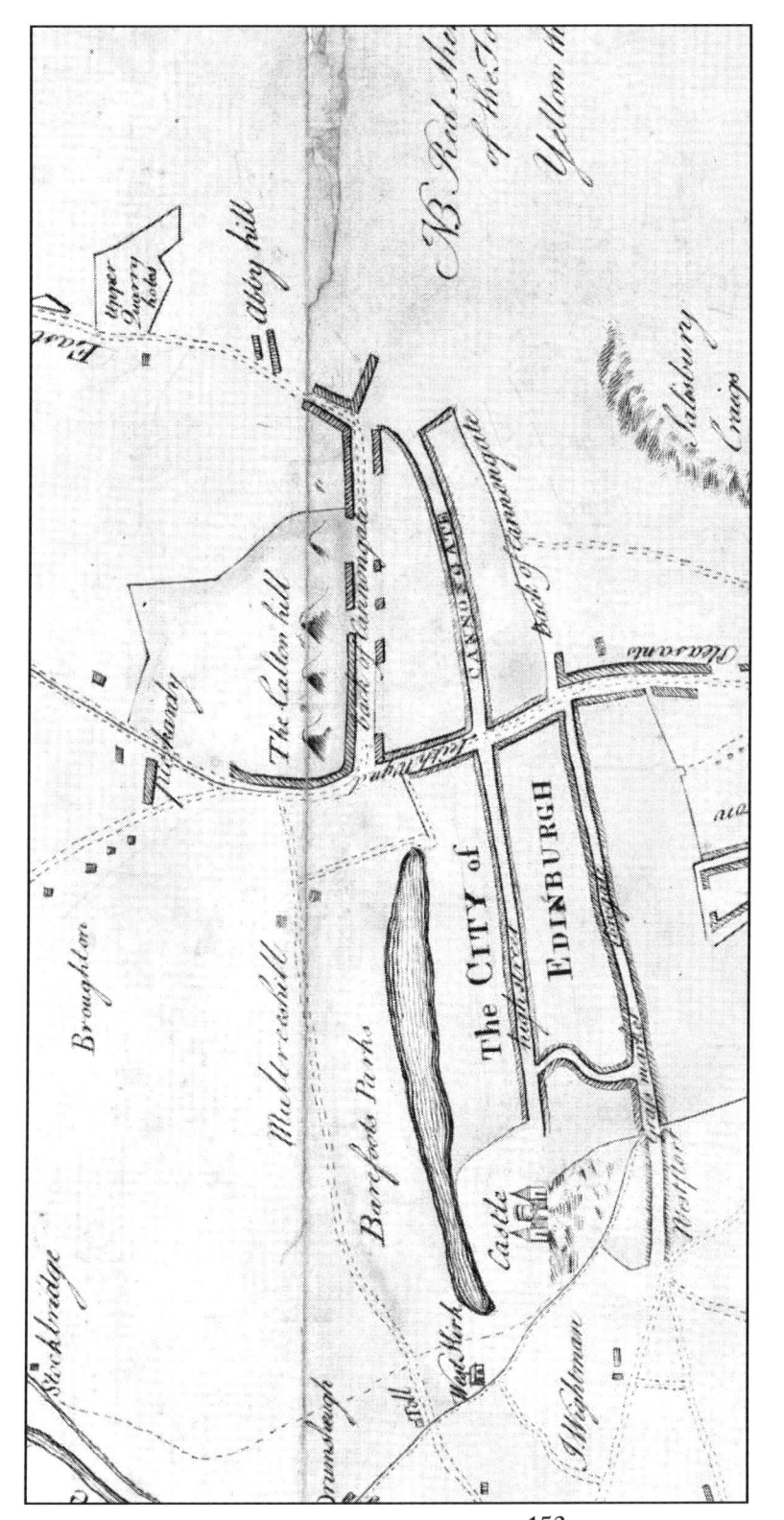

MAP A3 1759 (Richard Cooper) The weavers workshop was such a significant feature that it even showed up (complete with the name 'pickardy') in this map of Edinburgh and Leith.

A Brief & Incomplete Family History

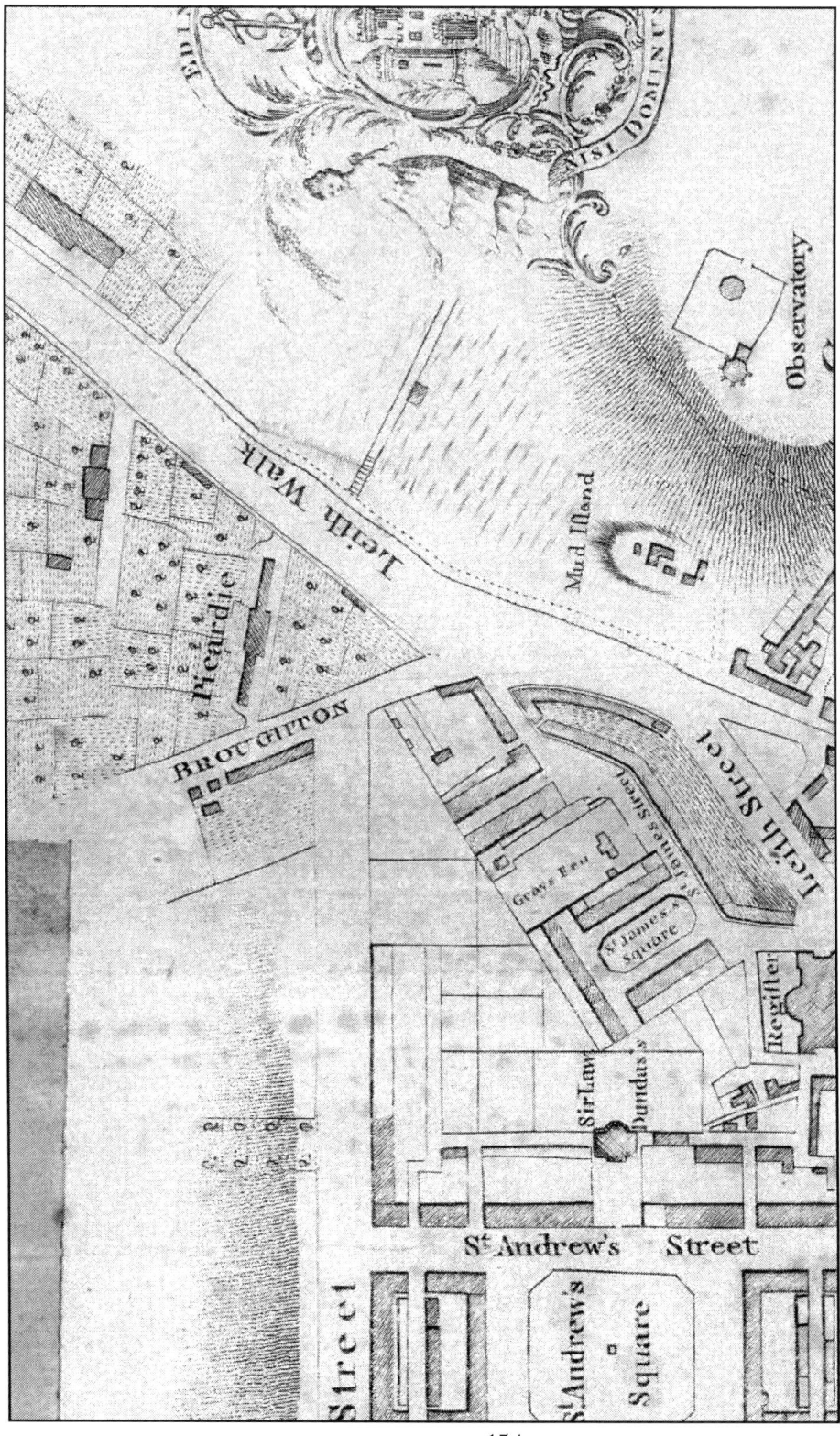

MAP A4 – 1787 (Daniel Lizars). By the 1780s the 'New Town' was expanding to the north of the 'Old Town'. Even so, this map shows the 'Picardie' workshops. As the original grant included 5 acres we can assume the orchards shown around the weaver's building also belonged to the weavers. There is a separate building to the north which may have been the bake house run by the weavers.

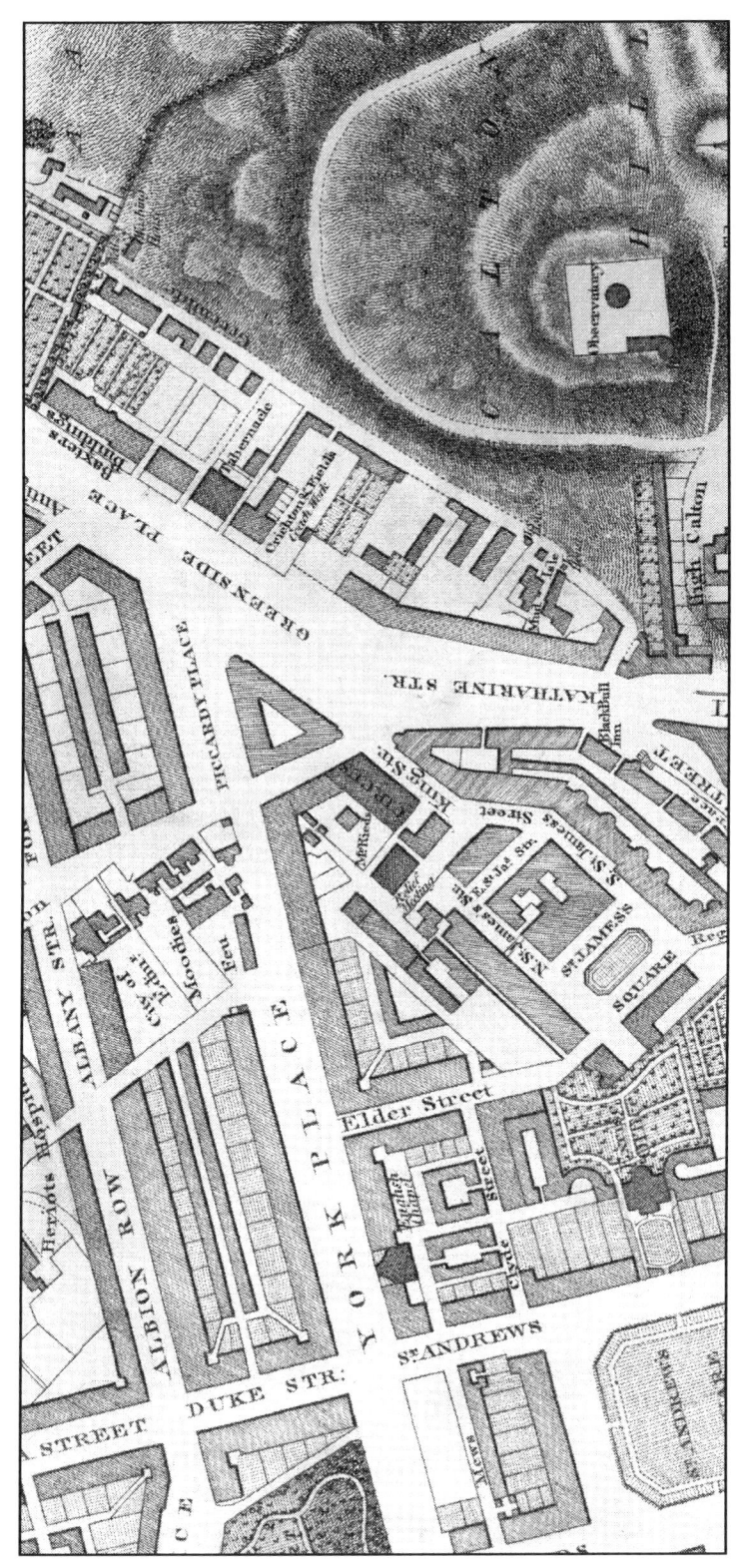

MAP A5 – 1804 (John Ainslie). By the early 1800s the expansion of Edinburgh 'New Town' had extended to the area to the north of the city walls, and the buildings and orchards of the weavers had disappeared. All that remained was the name 'Picardy Place'. Even today, the name remains, even if it is little more than a traffic roundabout.

A Brief & Incomplete Family History

Bethnal Green, London

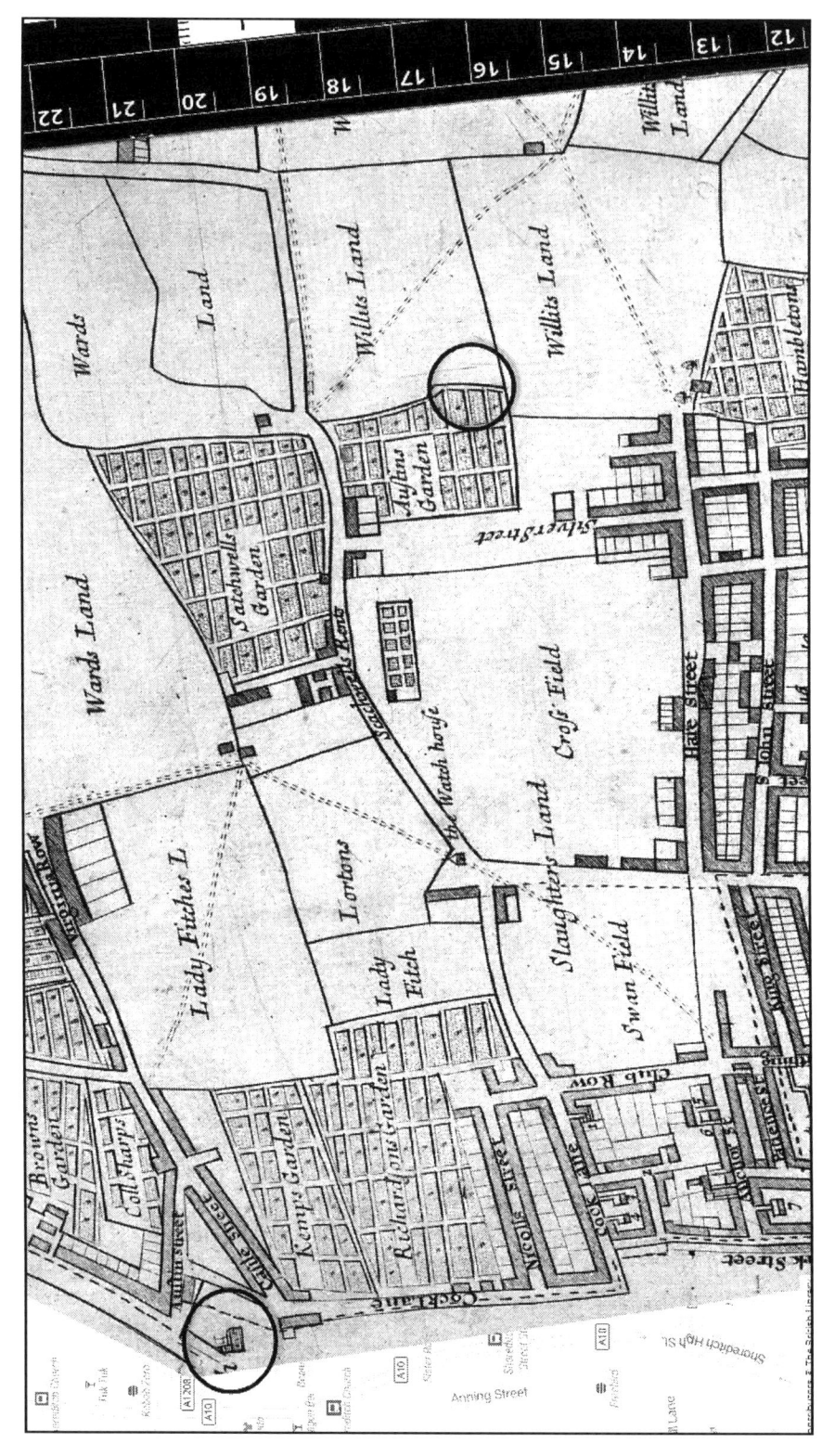

MAP B1 – 1720. Part of the parish map of St. Dunstan in the East.

St. Dunstan is the oldest church in East London and halfway between London Bridge and the Tower of London.

The church was largely destroyed during the Second World War and is now a public garden.

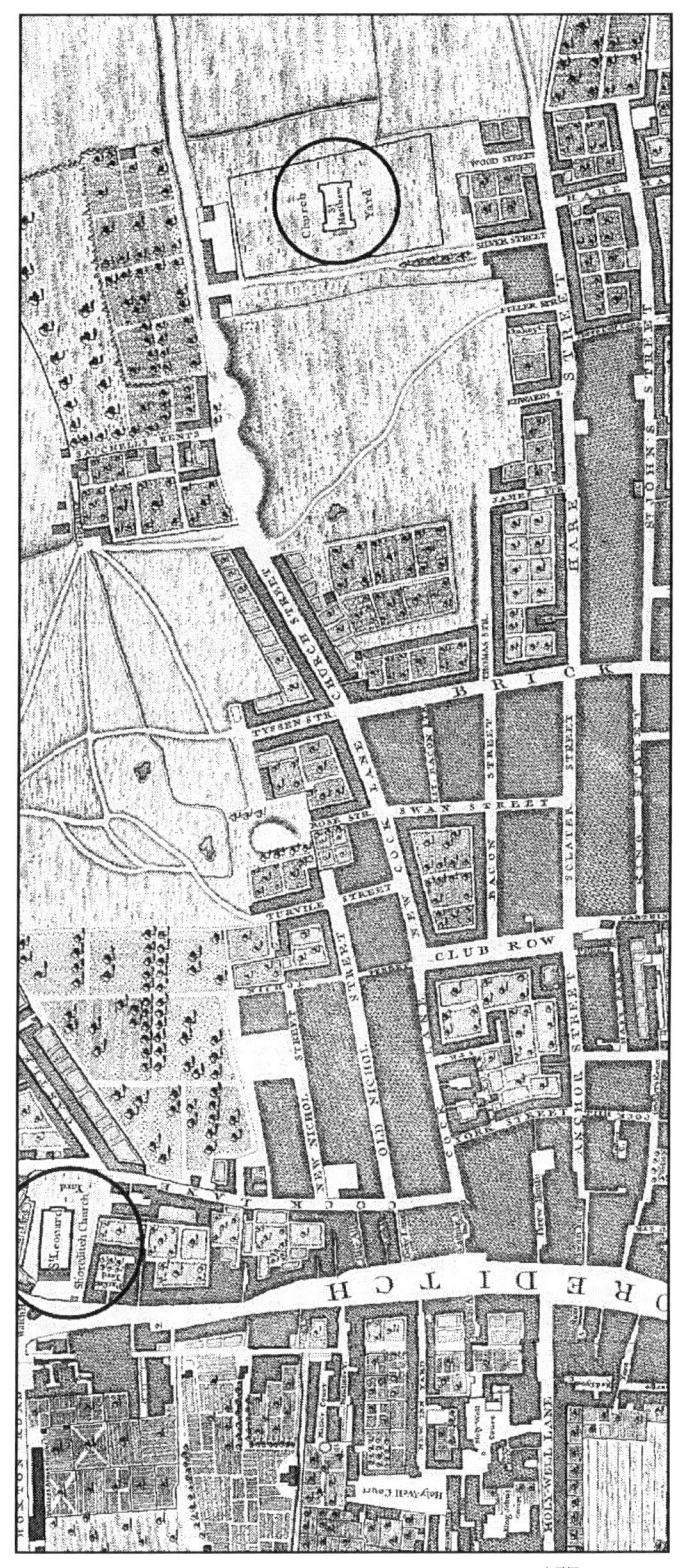

MAP B2 - 1746 (John Rocque) *map showing west Bethnal Green. The two churches of St. Leonard (top left) and St. Matthews (right) have now been built and are circled.*

The area around 'Nichol Street has been built up since the last map of the area. A 'new' Nichol Street has been built to the north and the original Nichol Street has been renamed 'Old Nichol Street'. Many of the streets in this area will have the name 'Nichol' after the lawyer who bought the land originally in the 17th Century. There is also new housing in Turvile Street, Club Row, Bacon Street and Sclater Street.

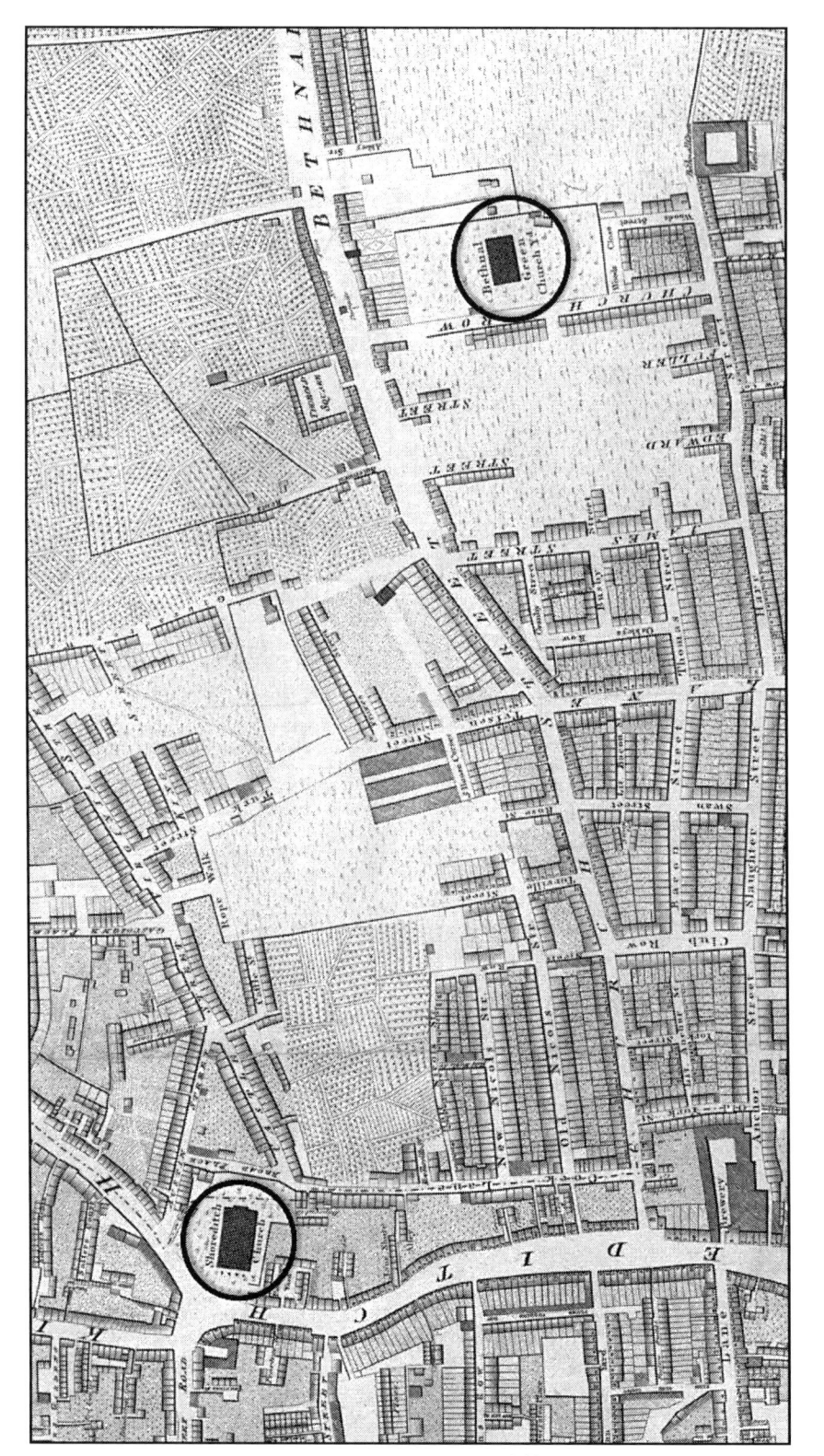

MAP B3 – 1799 (Horwood) Map of west Bethnal Green.

St. Leonard's church is circled in the top left corner–St. Matthew's church is circled on the right. In the 50 years since the last map of London, the residential housing of Spitalfields and Shoreditch has expanded to the west of St. Matthew.

We know that some of Paul's children lived in James Street, Thomas Street and Edward Street at some stage of their lives.

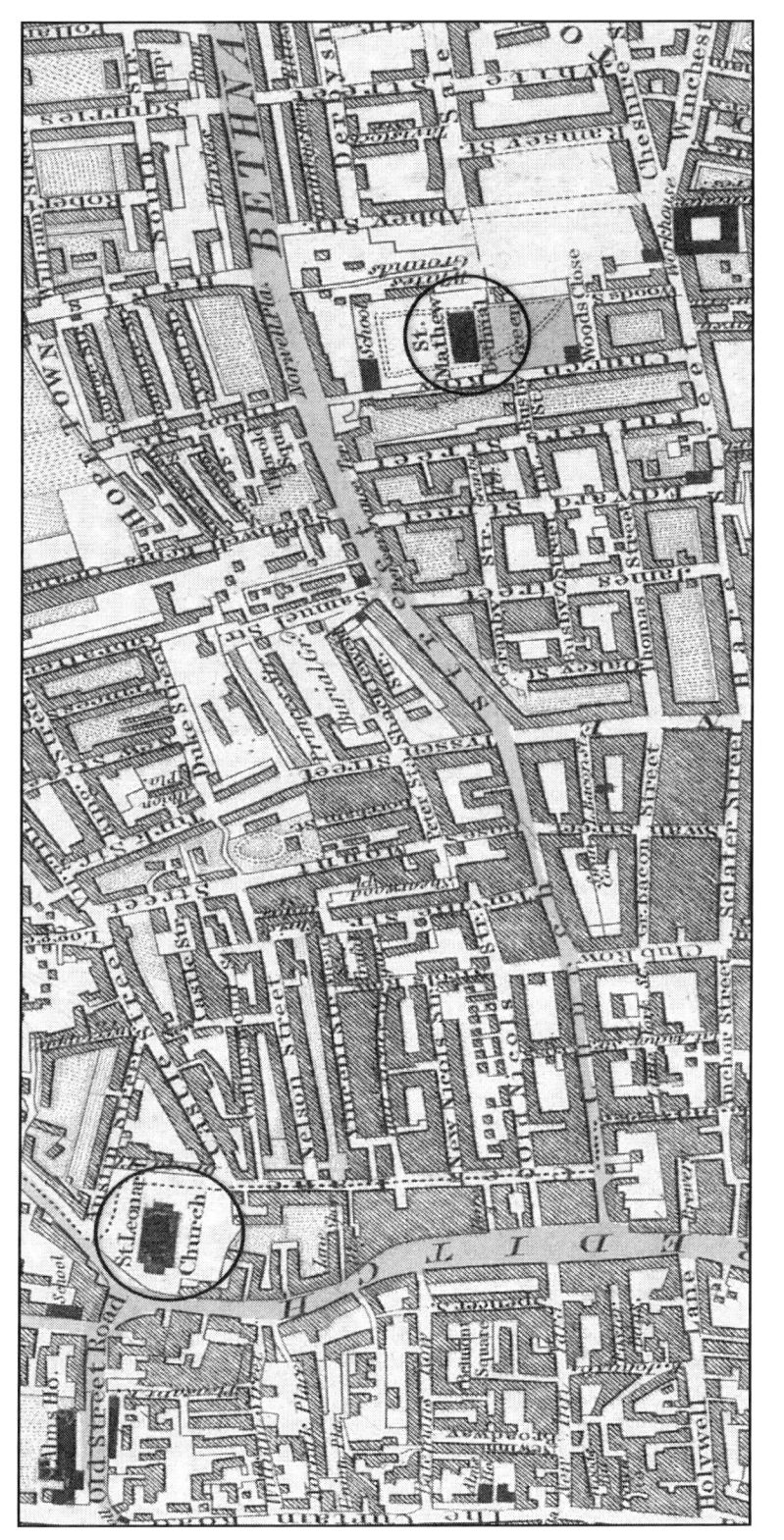

MAP B4 – 1827 (Greenwood) The area to the west of St Matthew's church had been extensively developed right up to Church Row.

The houses in James Street, Thomas Street and Edward Street are arranged around small courtyards. Over time the courtyards are also built in, leading to a maze of small houses and alleyways.

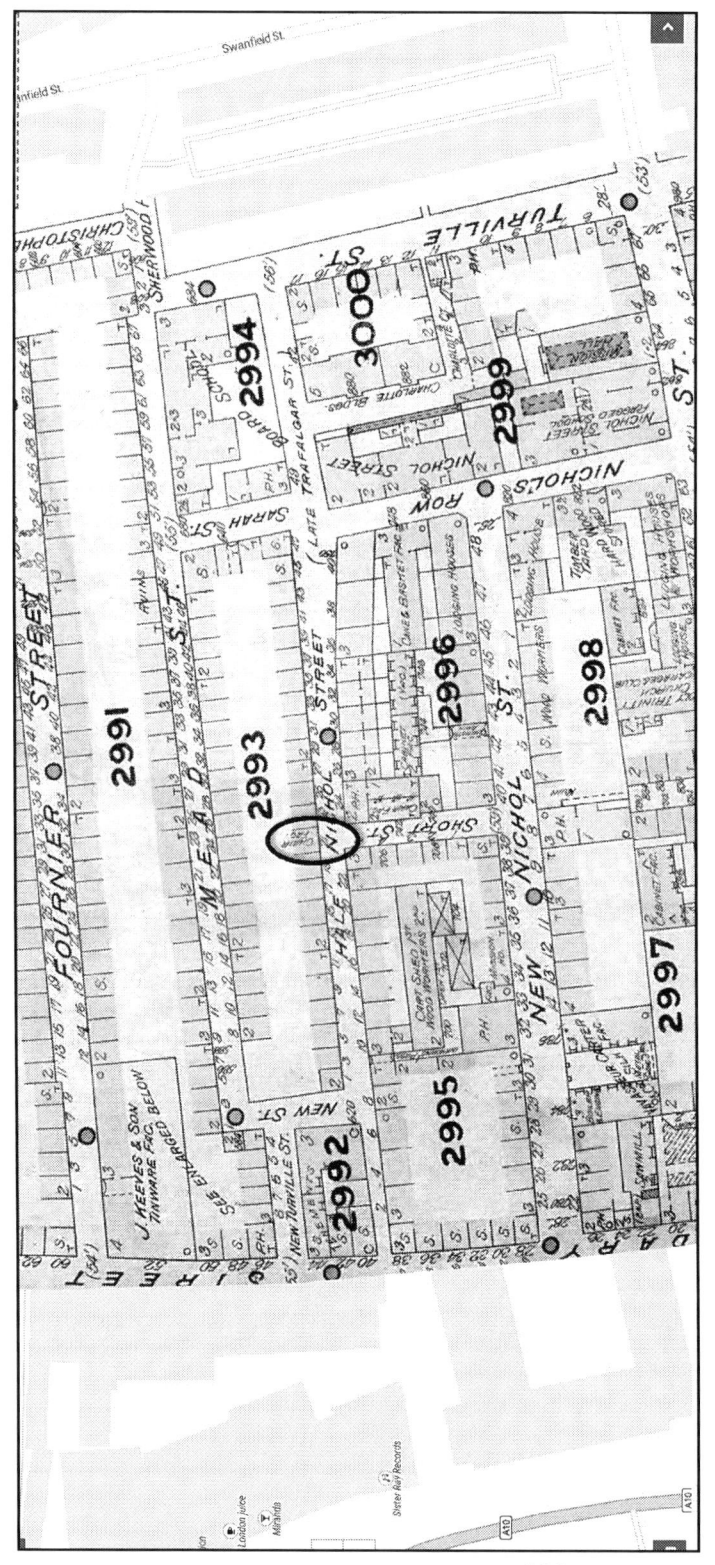

MAP B5 – 1890 (Fire Safety Insurance Map). This is the only detailed map of the 'Old Nichol'. The ringed area shows the location of 21, Half Nichol Street where George, Elizabeth and their family lived.

Some of the family later lived in Trafalgar Street, an extension of Half Nichol Street.

The key to the map gives details of the building heights, construction and roof materials (2 storey, tiled roof etc.)

A Brief & Incomplete Family History

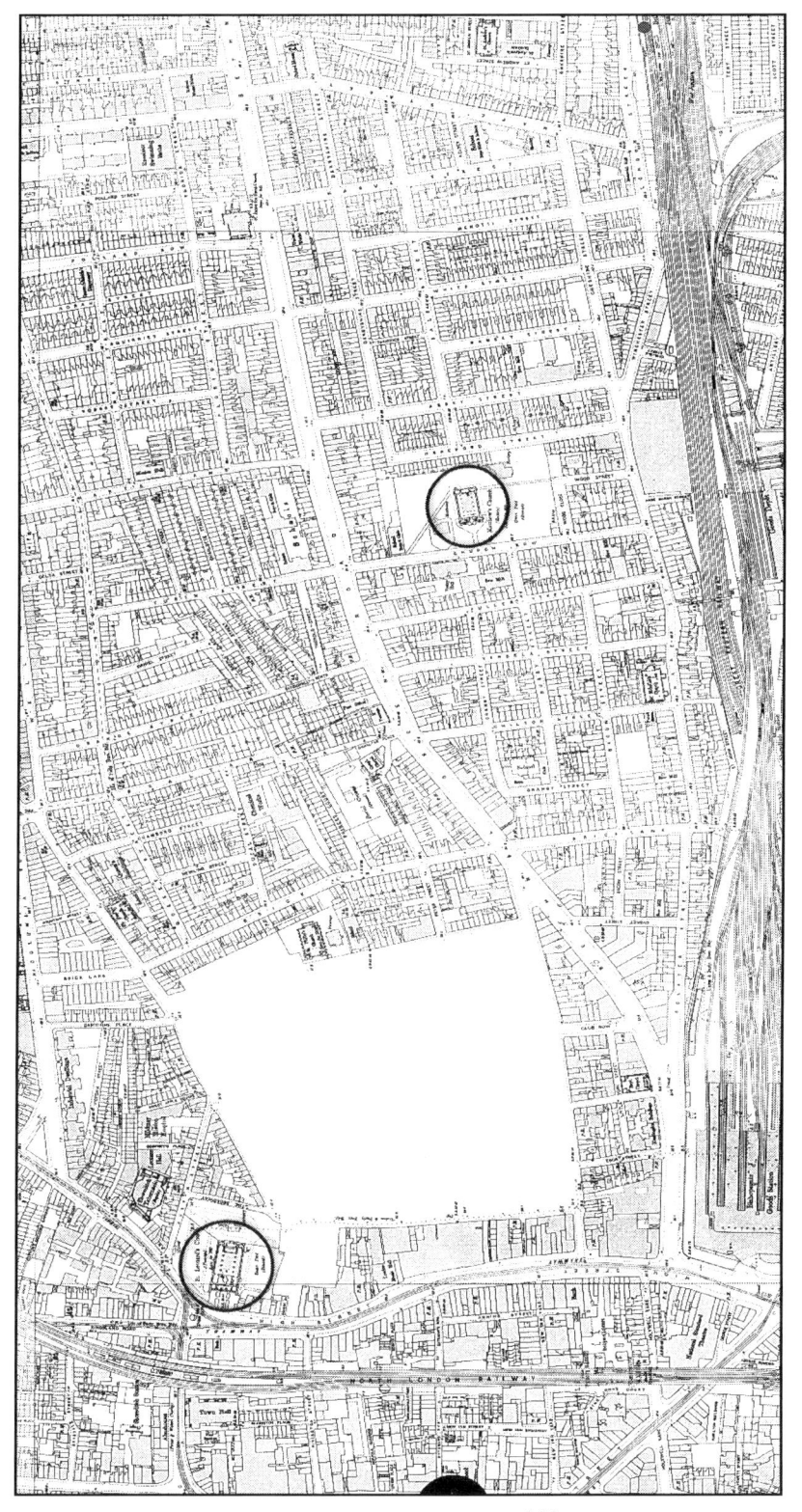

MAP B6 – 1893 *(ordnance Survey) The area surrounding the 'Old Nichol' district showing the extent of the demolition by the LCC.*

A Brief & Incomplete Family History

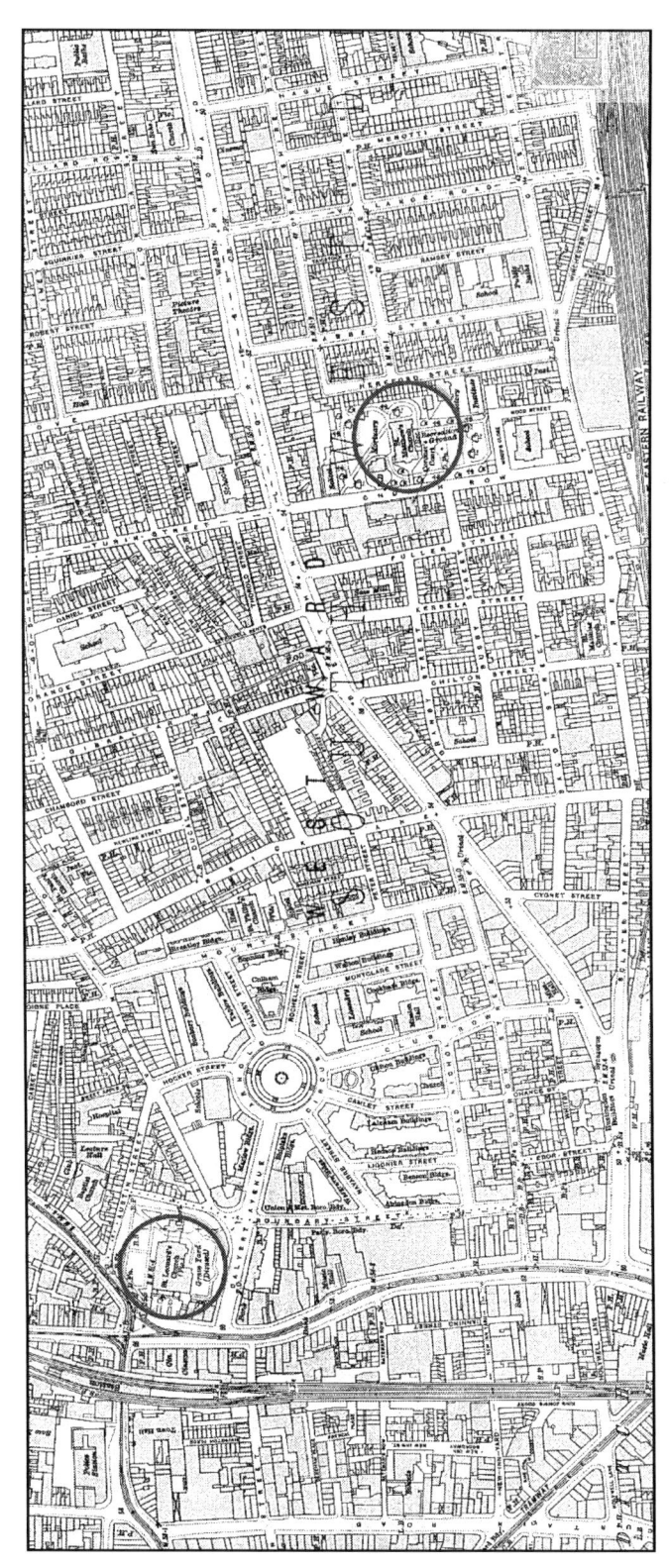

MAP B7 – 1905 (Ordnance Survey). The Boundary Road estate now fills the space where the 'Old Nichol' used to be.

A Brief & Incomplete Family History

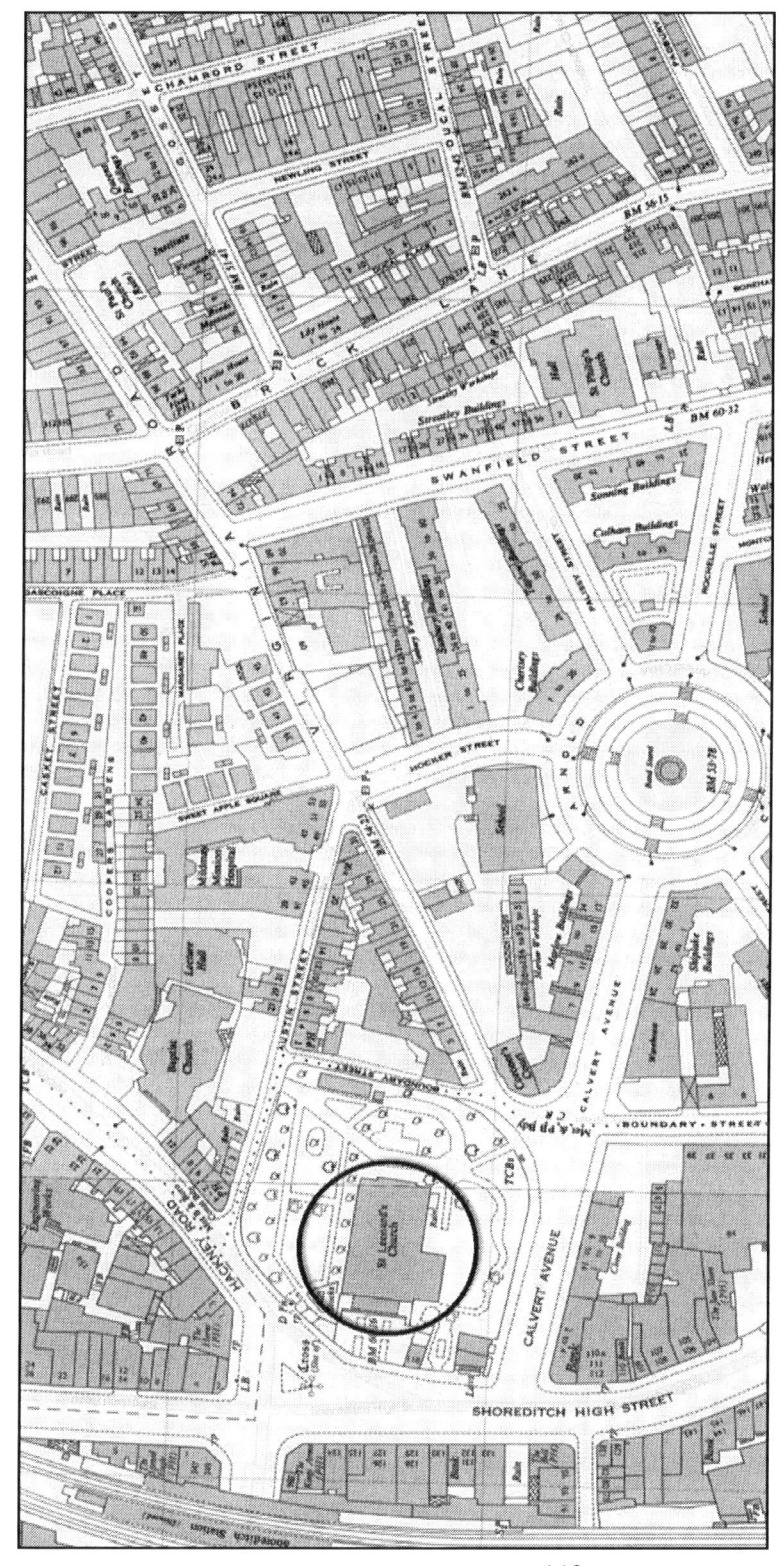

MAP B8 – 1960 (Ordnance Survey). The Boundary Road Estate as it currently is. The circular area is Arnold Circus and has a bandstand at the centre.

A Brief & Incomplete Family History

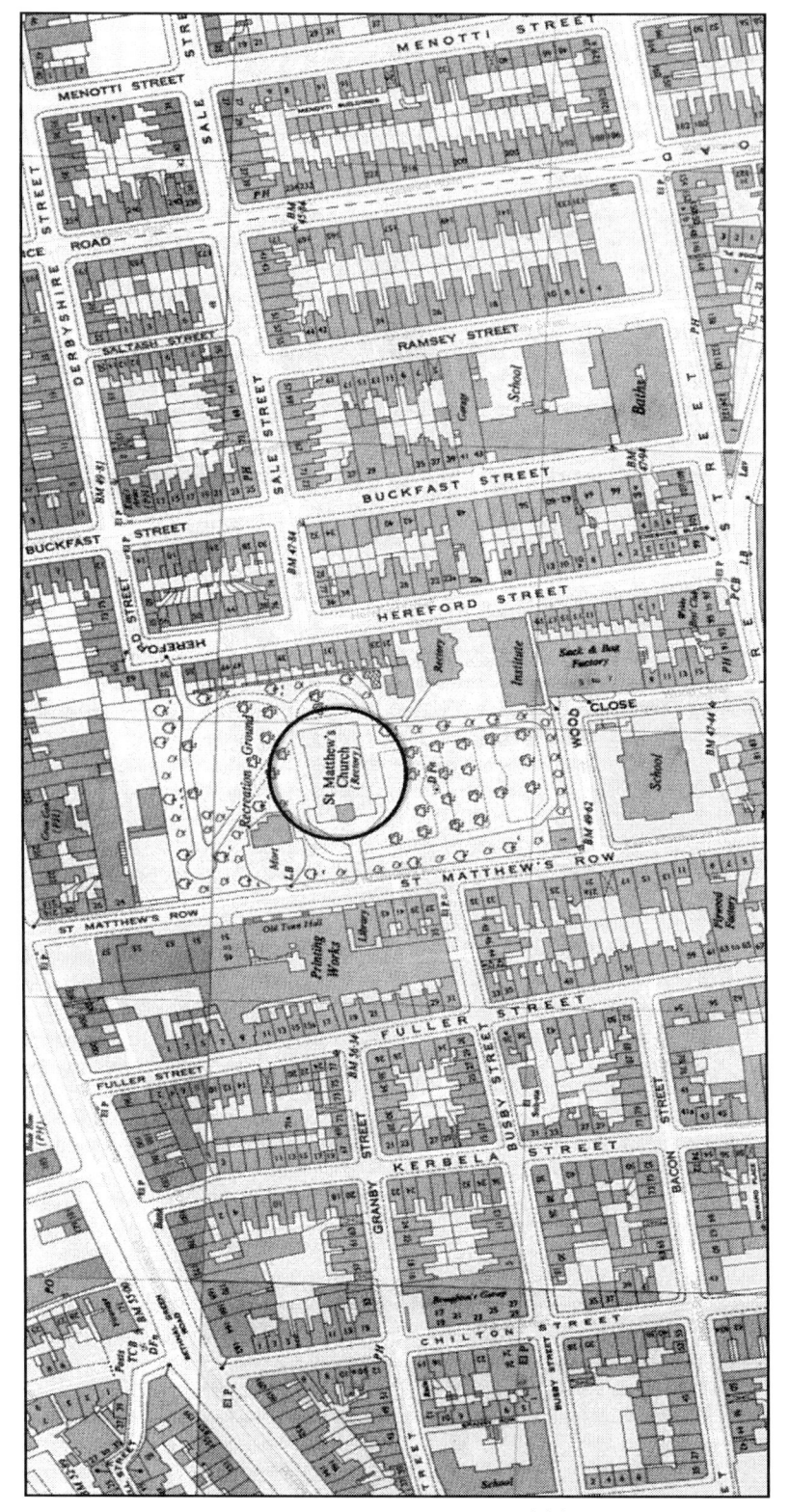

MAP B9 – 1960 (Ordnance Survey). The area around St. Matthew's Church in Bethnal Green as it is today. The graveyard was converted into a park. There is little in the surrounding area that remains from Victorian times.

Threadneedle Street (Bank), London

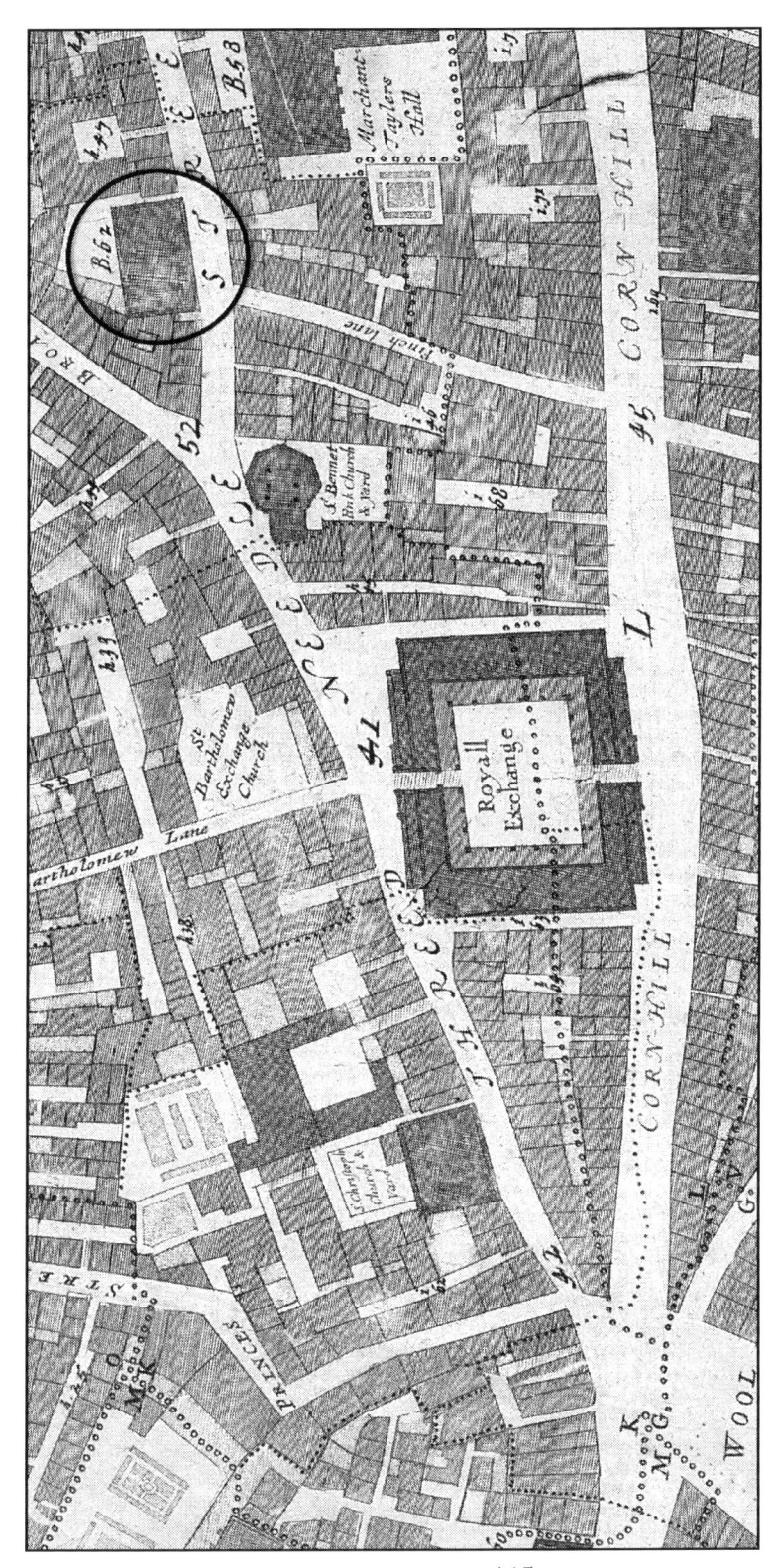

MAP C1 – 1676. The earliest map showing the location of the French Protestant Church in Thread Needle Street. The building shown here (circled) was rebuilt following the Great Fire of London in 1666. Before the Huguenots built their church, they used an existing medieval chapel (the Chapel of St. Anthony's Hospital) on the same site.

A Brief & Incomplete Family History

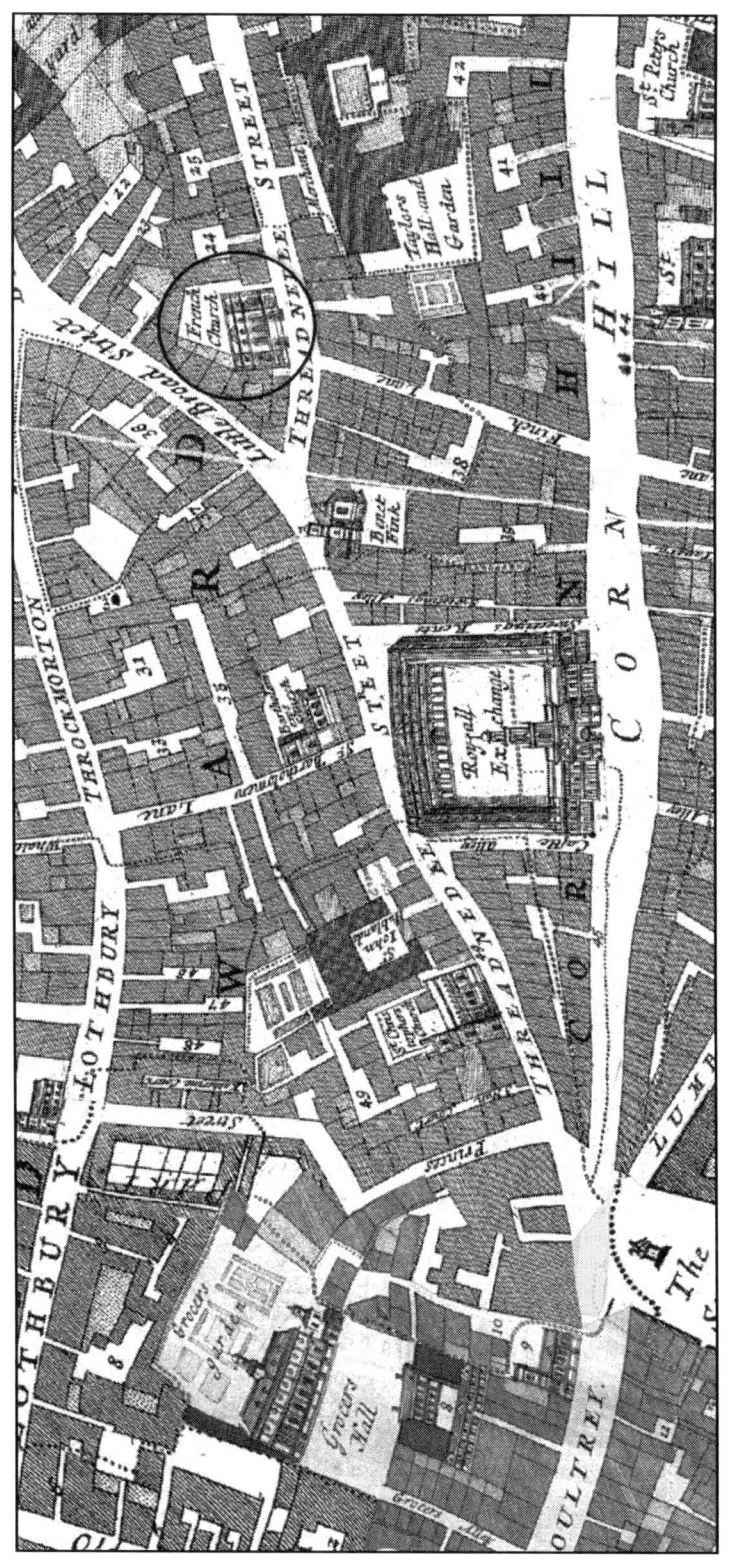

MAP C2 – 1720 (Blome & Strype). The location of the French Church is clearly shown in Threadneedle Street. The original Royal Exchange building was destroyed during the Great Fire in 1666. This Royal Exchange building survived until 1821 when it too burnt down.

A Brief & Incomplete Family History

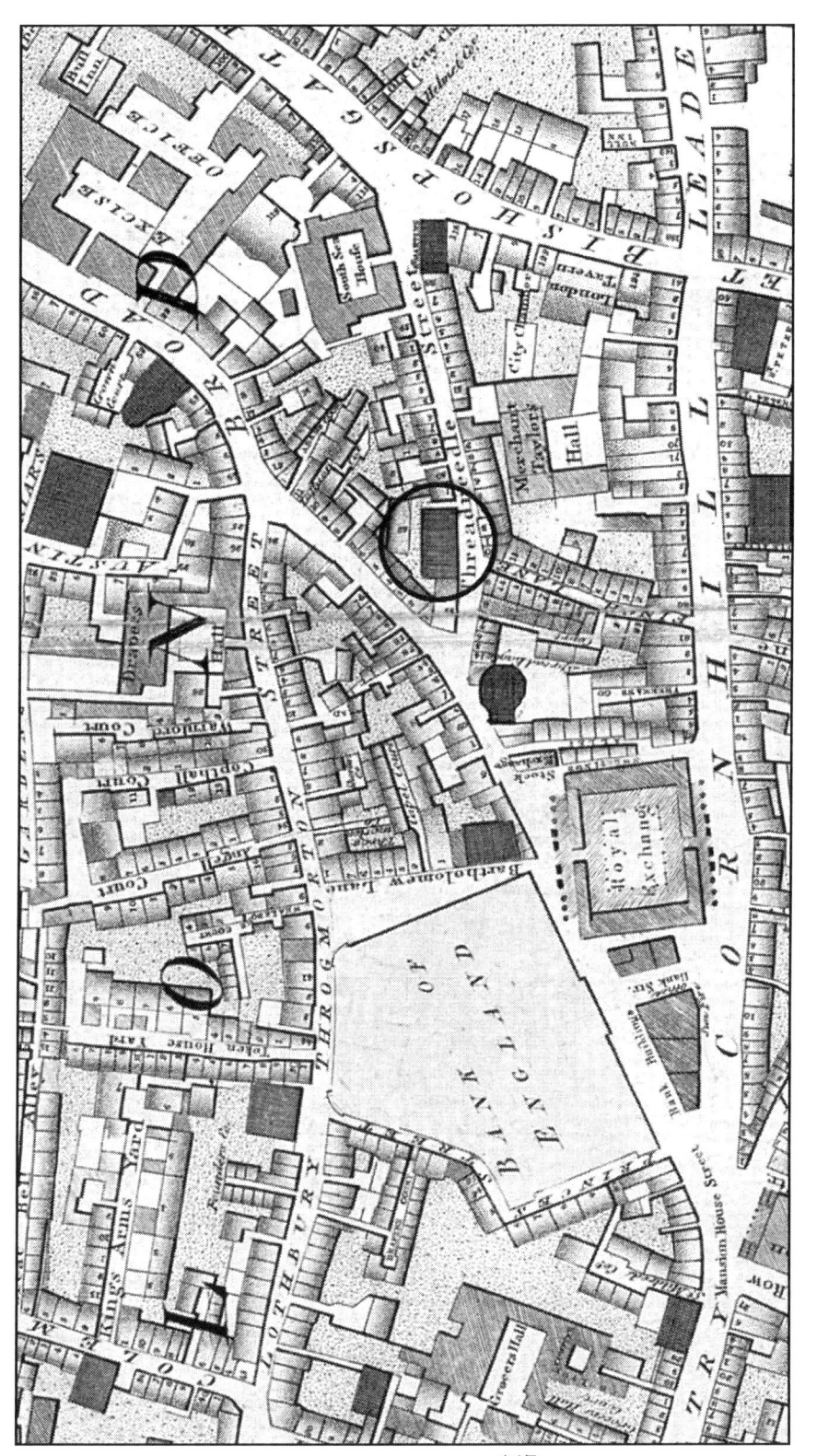

MAP C3 – 1792 (Horewood). The big change to the area by 1792 was the new building for the Bank of England.

When the Bank first opened in 1694, it was based in Cheapside. The Bank moved to Threadneedle Street in 1734 and eventually took over the land shown above.

The structure of the Bank of England remained more or less untouched until it was demolished and a new building erected by architect Sir Herbert Baker, between 1925 and 1939. However, Sir John Sloane's outer wall remains in place to this day.

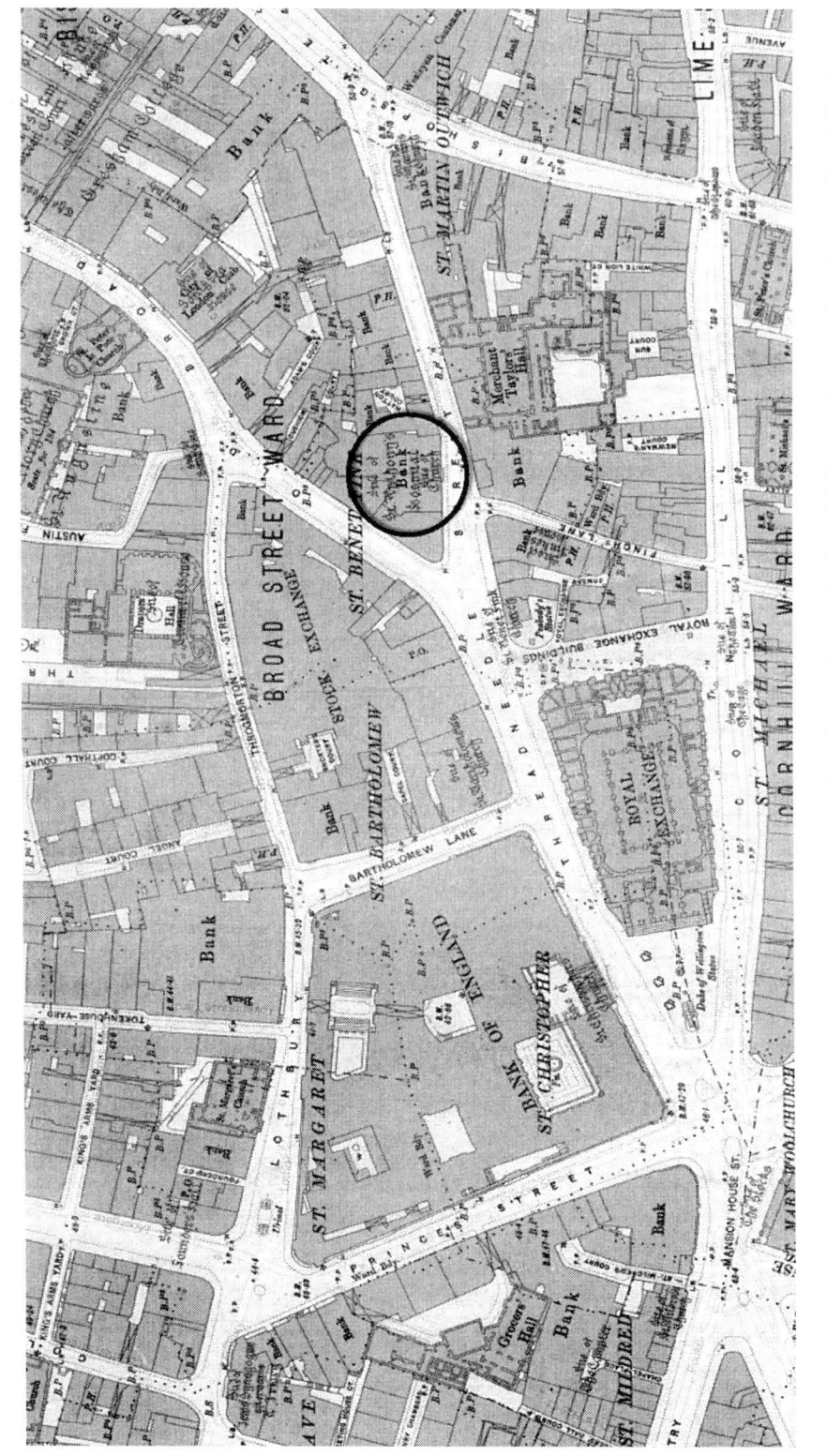

MAP C4 – 1896 (Ordnance Survey) The French Protestant Church was demolished in 1841 to make way for the new Royal Exchange building. There had been two previous Royal Exchanges, both destroyed by fire.

By this stage the majority of French Protestants in London were in the Soho area so the congregation at Threadneedle Street had declined.

However, the location of the Church is still clearly shown in the 1896 Ordnance Survey map, when the site was occupied by a Bank. The current building is different to the buildings on either side so it is easy to identify the original plot occupied by the Church.

A Brief & Incomplete Family History

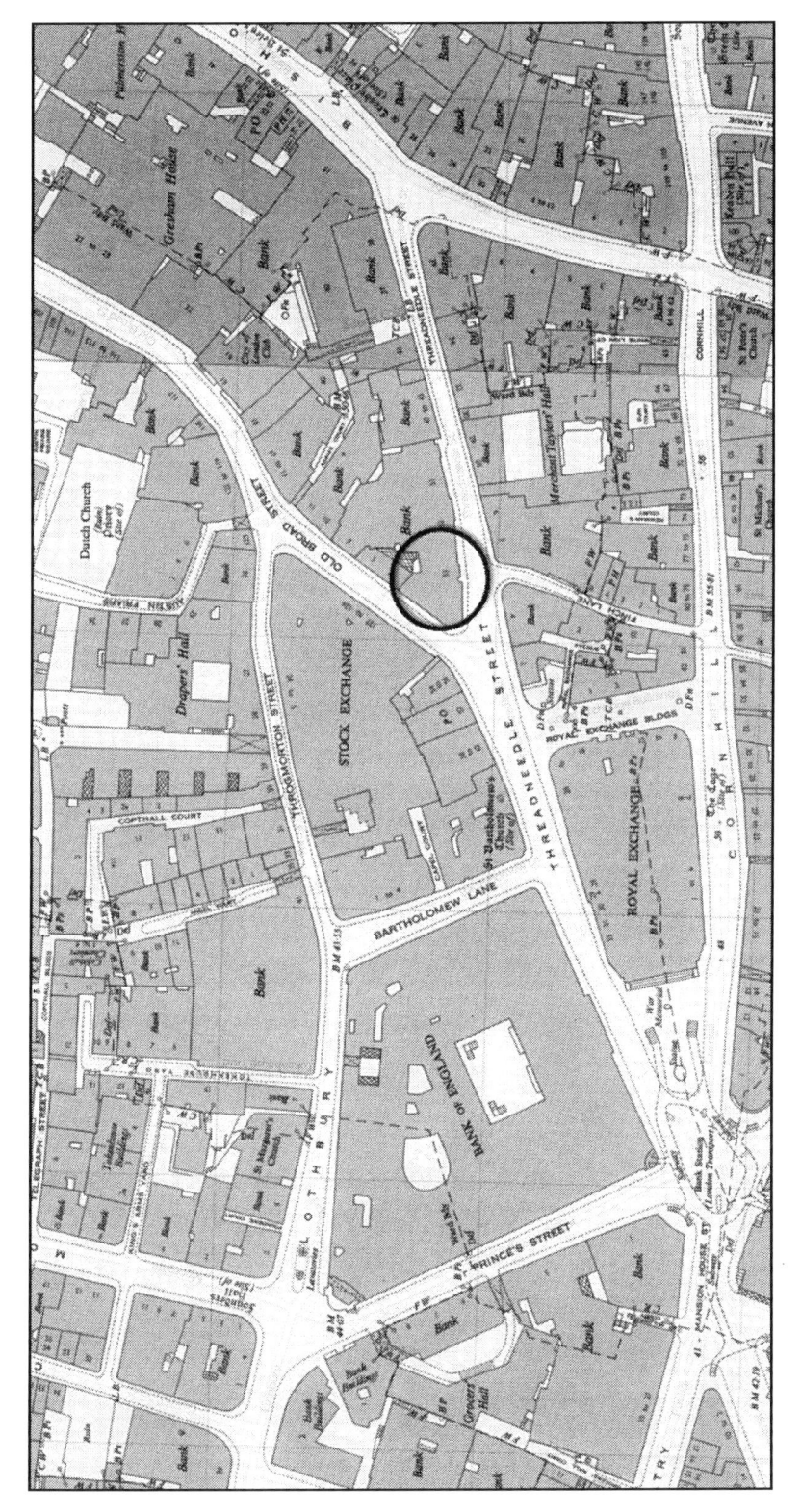

*MAP C5 - 1960 (**Ordnance Survey**) There has been lots of new building work since the 1960 survey, as can be seen in the photographs below. However, the site of the demolished Church was is still evident.*

A Brief & Incomplete Family History

Sample Census Forms

1841 Census. Contains very little information by comparison with later forms. The originals are badly discoloured and faded, making them difficult to transcribe. Headings are House number, Uninhabited or Building/Inhabited (?), Name, Sex & Age, Profession and where born.

170

1881 Census. Although it does not appear to have much more information than earlier forms, a few extra columns and the information across the top of the form allows much better analysis by area and district.

1921 Census (the last available). The form has greatly increased width, allowing more expansive answers. Relationships between members of the household are easier to understand, including children who have died. The columns on the right are only to simplify data collection and don't increase the information collected.

Printed in Great Britain
by Amazon